THE EVOLUTION OF MYTH IN GARCIA MARQUEZ FROM *LA HOJARASCA* TO *CIEN AÑOS DE SOLEDAD*

HISPANIC STUDIES COLLECTION

EDICIONES UNIVERSAL. Miami, Florida, 1981

ROBERT LEWIS SIMS

THE EVOLUTION OF MYTH IN GARCIA MARQUEZ FROM *LA HOJARASCA* TO *CIEN AÑOS DE SOLEDAD*

P. O. Box 450353 (Shenandoah Station)
Miami, Fl. 33145. USA.

To my mother and Anne II

INTRODUCTION

I

García Márquez' literary prominence dates from 1967 with the publication of *Cien años de soledad*. In the period from 1955 to 1967, he wrote *La hojarasca* (1955), *El coronel no tiene quien le escriba* (1961), *Los funerales de la Mamá Grande* (1962), *La mala hora* (1962) and *Cien años de soledad*.[1] García Márquez was writing during a period of political unrest in Colombia. From 1948 to about 1963, Colombia was embroiled in a bloody phenomenon known as «la violencia» in which several hundred thousand people died. This political turmoil represented an ongoing process from the post-independence period, and it left its mark on him: «Yo entonces tenía 22 ó 23 años (1950), había escrito *La hojarasca*, tenía en la cabeza la nebulosa de *Cien años de soledad* y me dije: 'Cómo voy yo a seguir trabajando en este terreno mítico y con este tratamiento poético, en estas circunstancias que estamos viviendo. Parece una evasión.' Fue una decisión política, equivocada, creo ahora. Decidí acercarme más a la actualidad del momento colombiano y escribí *El coronel no tiene quien le escriba* y *La mala hora*.»[2] Like many Latin American novelists, he felt compelled to react to the immediate political situation, to document reality in a committed manner. He responded to a problem which has plagued Latin America for more than a century, which was «la violencia organizada desde el poder, los conservadores arrasaban pueblos, poblaciones enteras, armaban las policías y el ejército y a sus partidarios para aterrorizar a los liberales que eran mayoría y poder mantenerse en el poder.»[3] Because of the impact of the situation, many writers «sintieron la necesidad de contarlo y entonces aparecieron en cuatro a cinco años más de 50 novelas que es lo que se llama ahora la novela de la violencia en Colombia.»[4] García Márquez' two novels, *El coronel no tiene quien le escriba* and *La mala hora*, constitute his contribution to this political situation.

Initially, however, he had embarked on another path which would ultimately prove decisive: «Mira, yo empecé bien, empecé por donde debía. El mismo tratamiento mítico de *Cien años de soledad* está en *La hojarasca*.»⁵ He soon realized that if he continued to write political novels, «por ese camino no iba a ninguna parte: tenía que escribir un libro cada vez que cambiara la situación, como se hace justamente con los reportajes. Creo que tuve más madurez política y me di cuenta que no era cierto que el tratamiento mítico fuera una evasión. Entonces me lancé a hacer *Cien años de soledad* como lo hice.»⁶ This new depiction of reality required a different approach which would break the bonds of the past. As D.P. Gallagher explains: «If a novel is a fictive construct, a creation, and not a mirror that meticulously reflects reality, it follows that there is not much point in measuring up the events it depicts against real known facts. Contemporary Latin American novelists have allowed themselves therefore to unleash their imaginations, and sheer fantasy is a prominent ingredient of contemporary Latin American fiction.»⁷ This change in García Márquez takes place in *FMG:* «De ahí que los libros que resulten comunes en cuanto a lenguaje sean *La hojarasca* y *Cien años de soledad*, por un lado y, por otro, *El coronel no tiene quien le escriba* y *La mala hora*. En el libro de cuentos *Los funerales de la Mamá Grande* hay ambas cosas, porque los cuentos son un poco deshechos, material que me iba quedando con el que logré armar un libro.»⁸

In this new orientation, he sought to combine both paths into a more comprehensive view of Latin American reality which would transcend the narrow bounds explored by the previous generation of novelists. García Márquez was striving to create a more universal vision which would extend beyond Colombia and Latin America to encompass man in general, and he returned to his mythic approach in *H:*

> Mira, lo que pasa es que se me abrió una idea más clara del concepto de realidad. El realismo inmediato de *El coronel no tiene quien le escriba* y *La mala hora* tiene un radio de alcance. Pero me di cuenta que la realidad es también los mitos de la gente, es las creencias, es sus leyendas; son su vida cotidiana e intervienen en sus triunfos y en sus fracasos. Me di cuenta que la realidad no era sólo los policías que llegan matando gente, sino también toda la mitología, todas las leyendas, todo lo que forma parte de la vida de la gente y todo eso hay que incorporarlo. Te hablo de los presagios, de la telepatía, de muchas de esas creen-

cias premonitorias en que vive inmersa la gente latinoamericana todos los días dándole interpretaciones supersticiosas a los objetos, a las cosas, a los acontecimientos. Interpretaciones, además que vienen de nuestros ancestros más remotos.[9]

This new concept of reality simultaneously rejects the narrow interpretation of the past and reincorporates it into a global vision more in tune with man's mythic impulses, and it transcends the limited, chronological dimensions to which human history has been confined. In an interview with Rosa Castro, García Márquez addressed this question:

> RC: No encontró dificultades para combinar en *Cien años de soledad* tanta fantasía como la que allí emplea con la realidad básica en que la obra se sustenta?

> GGM: No, porque vivimos en un continente donde la vida cotidiana está hecha de realidades y mitos, y nosotros nacemos y vivimos dentro de un mundo de realidades fantásticas.[10]

In the period from 1955 to 1967, García Márquez thus returned to a mythical approach which both denies and accepts the weight of the past, and permits him to transform it into a vision which is both old and new. His emphasis on myth holds the key to unlocking the plenary vision which he finally synthesizes in *CAS*.

García Márquez' fiction during this period moves towards reinstating myth as a collective experience expressed in written form; and Claude Lévi-Strauss' structural study of myth and his demonstration of «how myths think in men, unbeknown to them,» although not specifically designed to serve literary analysis, provide important analytical tools for studying García Márquez. In his approach to myth, Lévi-Strauss emphasizes its structure and function instead of trying to establish a comprehensive definition which would fit every situation. In terms of structure, a myth exhibits a triadic division which he compares to Saussurian linguistics. On the first level is found the individual telling of the myth (*parole*) which is located in time. The second is the form of the myth (*langue*) which can vary from version to version, and from which each telling derives. The third level constitutes the basic message, or code, which is transmitted intact from version to version, and which is supralinguistic. Lévi-Strauss says that «it is that double structure, altogether historical and ahistorical, which explains how myth , while pertaining to the realm of *parole* and calling for an explanation as such, as well as to that of *langue* in which it is expressed, can also be an absolute entity on a third level which, though it remains linguistic by nature, is nevertheless distinct from the other two.»[11] He states that myth, like language, is composed of constituent units, and the third level, which emits the myth's fundamental message, is composed of what he calls gross constituent units or mythemes. These are the elements which are common to all the variants of a myth, and they are derived by comparing all the versions of a myth and make up the equivalent of the original version of the myth. These basic units are not isolated relations, but bundles of such relations which share the same functional trait. They can be reordered from telling to telling, but their message remains the same. An example will illustrate Lévi-Strauss' method. Sophocles' *Oedipus Rex* is one version of the total Oedipus myth, and it is situated in time (*parole*). But the structure of the myth (*langue*) is also timeless because «it explains the present and the past as well as the future.»[12] Each time the myth is retold, it combines *parole* and *langue* and then transcends both to reach the supralinguistic level on which the basic message cannot be altered by any particular version.

For Lévi-Strauss, the structural study of myth also involves the premise that mythical thought, which he sees operating in primitive societies, employs a logic as rigorous as that of modern science. He says that the function of myth «is to provide a logical model capable of overcoming a contradiction.»[13] Myth continuously offers solutions to problems, for its timelessness allows its basic message to be reformulated in a theoretically endless series of versions. In order to distinguish between mythical and scientific thought, Lévi-Strauss draws a contrast between two kinds of workmen, the engineer and the *bricoleur*. The engineer defines his project, chooses the precise equipment and materials needed for it, and carries it out in the most efficient way possible. The *bricoleur* (who may be defined as a kind of Jack-of-all-trades), confronted with a comparable task, carries it out in a much less direct fashion. His set of equipment and materials is also finite, but heterogeneous because «what it contains bears no relation to the current project, or indeed to any particular project, but is the contingent result of all the occasions there have been to renew or enrich the stock or to maintain it with the remains of previous constructions or destructions.»[14] The *bricoleur* can perform a large number of tasks, but, unlike the engineer, «he does not subordinate each of them to the availability of raw materials and tools conceived and procured for the purpose of the project.»[15] As he works, the *bricoleur* «interrogates all the heterogeneous objects of which his treasury is composed to discover what each of them could 'signify' and so contribute to the definition of a set which has yet to materialize but which will ultimately differ from the instrumental set only in the internal disposition of its parts.»[16] The *bricoleur*'s method contains a built-in principle of expansion which mythical thought and narrative also exhibit; that is, they «are fundamentally comprehensive and plenary, or accruent.»[17] Mythical thought grasps the world «as both a synchronic and diachronic totality and the knowledge which it draws therefrom is like that afforded of a room by mirrors fixed on opposite walls, which reflect each other (as well as objects in the intervening space) although without being strictly parallel. A multitude of images forms simultaneously, none exactly like any other, so that no single one furnishes more than a partial knowledge of the decoration and furniture but the group is characterized by invariant properties expressing a truth.»[18]

The evolution of myth in García Márquez' works goes through several phases. In *H* he experiments with different time categories in order to create a timeless dimension in which Macondo can exist as a mythical place. In *FMG*, he employs two techniques which place his short story on the mythical threshold of *CAS*: 1) the *voz callejera* viewpoint; and 2) the *bricolage* structuring of the short story. The *voz callejera*, which is the perspective of legend and myth, transfers the story from a historical to a mythical, oral viewpoint. *FMG*'s *bricolage* structure liberates it from a chronological time sequence.

An examination of *CAS*'s macrostructure (its chapters) demonstrates how circularity and linearity, seemingly conflicting structural principles, combine to produce the novel's fluid form. *Bricolage*, because of its built-in principle of expansion, converts *CAS* into an open-structured novel more in tune with myth. A detailed study of the banana massacre episode reveals the operation of *bricolage* on *CAS*'s microstructural level. Attention then shifts to the role of the anonymous, omniscient narrator who closely resembles the storyteller of myth and the *bricoleur*. In addition, various techniques, such as the use of the preterite and imperfect, the repetition of 'haber de,' embedding, enumeration and hyperbole, establish *CAS*'s close relationship to the orality of mythical storytelling. A detailed study of the novel's family structure, which is one of the gross constituents of the myth of Macondo, demonstrates how the patriarchal family, which dominates in *H*, and the matriarchal family, which rules *FMG*, are combined into one unit in *CAS*. The Oedipus myth and the theme of incest are also incorporated into the *bricolage* family pattern. An examination of individual characters (José Arcadio Buendía, Ursula Iguarán, Colonel Aureliano Buendía and Melquíades) explores their status as mythical figures within the family structure. Finally, Macondo's position as a mythical place is considered. In *CAS*, where Macondo's complete history is revealed, its principal stages are analyzed to show their relationship to Colombian and Latin American history. García Márquez then transforms it into myth. By studying Macondo in relation to linear, circular and mythical time, its position as the *bricolage*, mythical center of the novel is confirmed.

Finally, I would like to thank those who contributed in one way or another to the realization of this book. To my wife, Anne, whose expert typing and proofreading were invaluable; to my colleague, Professor Ken Stackhouse, whose close reading of my manuscript and susggestions helped clarify it; to Virginia Commonwealth University whose grant allowed me to complete my work; and finally, and certainly not least, to Buddy LaBrenz, our incredibly efficient and patient secretary, whose masterful and expeditious typing deserves my highest praise.

NOTES

1. Hereafter I shall use the following abbreviations: *H* for *La hojarasca*, *FMG* for the short story «Los funerales de la Mamá Grande,» and *CAS* for *Cien años de soledad*.

2. E. González Bermejo, «Ahora 200 años de soledad,» *Oiga*, No. 392 (septiembre, 1970), p. 29.

3. *Ibid.*, p. 29.

4. *Ibid.*, p. 29.

5. *Ibid.*, p. 29.

6. *Ibid.*, p. 31.

7. D.P. Gallagher, *Modern Latin American Literature* (Oxford: Oxford University Press, 1973), p. 88.

8. Bermejo, p. 29.

9. *Ibid.*, p. 31.

10. Rosa Castro, «Con Gabriel García Márquez,» in: *Sobre García Márquez*, ed. Pedro Simon Martínez (Montevideo: Biblioteca de Marcha, 1971), p. 28.

11. Claude Lévi-Strauss, *Structural anthropology*, trans. Claire Jacobson and Brooke Grundfest Schoepf (Garden City, New York: Doubleday & Company, Inc., 1967), pp. 205-6.

12. *Ibid.*, p. 205.
13. *Ibid.*, p. 226.
14. Claude Lévi-Strauss, *The Savage Mind* (Chicago: The University of Chicago Press, 1970), p. 17.
15. *Ibid.*, p. 17.
16. *Ibid.*, p. 18.
17. Warner Berthoff, *Fictions and Events: Essays in Criticism and Literary History* (New York: E.P. Dutton & Co., Inc., 1971), p. 49.
18. *The Savage Mind*, p. 263.

OVERTURE TO MYTH: *LA HOJARASCA*

CHAPTER I

H (1955) began to draw more critical attention after *CAS* was published in 1967, but *H* nevertheless constitutes the first step in García Márquez' mythical evolution, which would culminate twelve years later in *CAS*. [1] García Márquez pointed out that «*La hojarasca* fue el primer libro que yo publiqué cuando vi que no podía escribir *Cien años de soledad*. Y ahora me doy cuenta que el verdadero antecedente de *Cien años de soledad* es *La hojarasca*.» [2] *H* presents a fragmented history of Macondo which will be completed in *CAS*. Vargas Llosa explains that many critics mistakenly believe that «la novela transcurre entre 1903 y 1928. Es inexacto: en 1903 llegan el médico y el Cachorro a Macondo, pero en *La hojarasca* se evocan (es verdad que de pasada) episodios muy anteriores a esa fecha. En realidad, la novela abraza (débilmente) un período que va desde la fundación de Macondo hasta 1928. Y, atendiendo a la frase profética de Isabel, se puede incluso sugerir que menciona el instante final del pueblo, de modo que los datos de esa ficción se extienden, dispersos, por el tiempo histórico completo de la realidad ficticia.» [3] Although *CAS* clarifies certain puzzling facets of Macondo's history in *H*, a simple cataloguing of these elements would deny *H*'s importance as the first crucial step in García Márquez' mythical evolution. In *H*, the three narrators remembering the past help develop temporal categories which contribute to the creation of myth: (1) time as a prolonged or continuous present; (2) time as memory and the dynamic fusion of the causal order in experience; and (3) time as a circular phenomenon. These categories are critical tools and, as such, do not arise naturally from the novel's structure. The prolonged present can be subdivided into four parts: (a) the half-hour duration of the novel; (b) a historical past spanning a period of twenty-five years (1903-1928); (c) a more imprecise past dating back to the founding of Macondo; (d) and finally, the subjective, psychological time of the narrators. These four divisions unfold simultaneously and combine to form the prolonged present.

The half-hour is alluded to at different points.[ʼ] This skeletal, external framework circumscribes the continuous present within whose boundaries García Márquez compresses the doctor's story and Macondo's history. The prolonged present erases the «fronteras entre el 'hoy' y el 'entonces',» and it corresponds to the «tiempo interior, psicológico, que se desenvuelve en su profundidad, acicateado por asociaciones y juegos de la memoria no regida por la voluntad.»[⁵ʼ] When the Colonel hears the train whistle, he says «Son las dos y media» (p. 29), and objective time disappears: «*Las dos y media del 12 de setiembre de 1928; casi la misma hora de ese día de 1903 en que este hombre se sentó por primera vez a nuestra mesa y pidió hierba para comer.* Adelaida le dijo aquella vez: '¿Qué clase de hierba, doctor?' Y él, con su parsimoniosa voz de rumiante, todavía perturbada por la nasalidad: 'Hierba común, señora. De esa que comen los burros'» (p. 29). Remembered time coexists with the present. At another point, he refers to his first meeting with the doctor and says that «no sabía que esa tarde estaban comenzando las cosas que hoy concluyen» (p. 50). Isabel's distinction between objective and subjective time places past events in the continuous present: «Si el *tiempo de adentro* tuviera el mismo ritmo del de *afuera*, ahora estaríamos a pleno sol, con el ataúd en la mitad de la calle. Afuera sería más tarde: sería de noche. Sería una pesada noche de setiembre con luna y mujeres sentadas en los patios, conversando bajo la claridad verde, y en la calle, nosotros, los tres renegados, a pleno sol de este setiembre sediento» (p. 60, italics mine). Her fear of what is going to happen and her memory place the doctor's arrival and the present situation in a synchronic relationship: «Desde hace veinticinco años, cuando este hombre llegó a nuestra casa... Y ahora, veinticinco años después, /the Colonel/ debe sentir que esto es apenas el cumplimiento de una tarea largamente premeditada, que habría llevado a cabo de todos modos, así hubiera tenido que arrastrar él mismo el cadáver por las calles de Macondo» (p. 17). The doctor's burial, as the external, temporal framework, is reduced to an absolute minimum, for García Márquez wishes to create «la ilusión de un bloque sólido, ininterrumpido» of events that unfold in the continuous present.[⁶] By continuously expanding the prolonged present within the limits of the half-hour, García Márquez keeps the reader equidistant from every past event.

In *H*, then, the half-hour represents the duration of the external time which can be called the «horizontal» present, whereas the «vertical,» continuous present reveals the past in all its inflectional forms.

It takes the form of individual frames, or projections of the narrators' minds by the use of temporal montage.[7] The following diagram illustrates the relationship between the two presents:

	Vertical, continuous present
	Doctor's story and Macondo's history
Horizontal present	The passage of the half-hour
following a linear path	Narrators remembering in the horizontal present
	Narrators' subjective time transferring events to vertical time

The particular configuration of this vertical line depends on the internal, subjective experience of each narrator.

The continuous present is related to the creation of myth in *H*. Since one of myth's characteristics is timelessness, García Márquez can insert the Greek myth of Antigone because it stands in vertical relation to the horizontal present. He puts the following epigraph at the beginning:

Y respecto del cadáver de Polinice, que miserablemente ha muerto, dicen que ha publicado un bando para que ningún ciudadano lo entierre ni lo llore, sino que insepulto y sin los honores del llanto, lo dejen para sabrosa presa de las aves que se abalancen a devorarlo. Ese bando dicen que el bueno de Creonte ha hecho pregonar por ti y por mí, quiere decir que por mí; y que me vendrá aquí para anunciar esa orden a los que no la conocen; y que la cosa se ha de tomar no de cualquier manera, porque quien se atreva a hacer algo de lo que prohibe será lapidado por el pueblo.

This passage from Sophocles describes the moment in which Antigone tells Ismene of Creon's decision concerning the funerals of Eteocles and Polyneces. *Antigone* parallels *H* in several ways, including the promise whose fulfillment will have dramatic consequences, the condemnation of the doctor, and above all the inflexible attitude of the Colonel. Their similarity «permite ver esta última como un intento de desarrollo, sutilmente elaborado, de la *visión trágica* de un presente social concreto, que llena de patetismo—al hacerla comprensiva—una expresión literaria que se proyecta en el hecho histórico que conocemos hoy bajo la denominación sociológica de la 'violencia colombiana'»[8] The structure of the Greek myth can be recreated in the doctor's story since its message, or code, remains the same from version to version. It is composed of mythemes which constitute the major elements common to all the versions. In *H*, García Márquez has modified the myth without changing its basic message. By placing the doctor's story and Macondo's history in the continuous present, they belong to a timeless realm in which Macondo can become a mythical place.

The continuous present also concerns time as memory and the dynamic fusion of the causal order in experience. In order to integrate the events in the vertical, continuous present, García Márquez uses a particular type of memory. Bergson and Proust identified two different forms of memory—voluntary and involuntary. Voluntary memory, based on habit, is subject to will and reason, and «enables us to develop a series of motor responses to present reality and to learn how to cope with our environment.»[9] Involuntary memory «occurs when a chance event disturbs the equilibrium established by habit and brings back the complete image of a past moment still stamped with 'a date and place.'»[10] Proust believed that the present moment of experience, a taste, a sensation, or an odor, could trigger the associative process leading to the «region of 'pure memory' which then unfolds to our minds the entire past with all its details preserved in their nascent state.»[11]

In *H*, García Márquez uses involuntary memory. In the first chapter, the boy hears the train whistle which sets this process in motion: «Vuelve a pitar el tren, cada vez más distante, y pienso de repente: 'Son las dos y media.' Y recuerdo que a esta hora (mientras el tren pita en la última vuelta del pueblo) los muchachos están haciendo filas en la escuela para asistir a la primera clase de la tarde. 'Abraham,' pienso» (pp. 15-16). In chapter five, it is the peculiar odor of the stifling room which activates the same phenomenon: «Si me vendaran los ojos, si me cogieran de la mano y me dieran veinte vueltas por el pueblo y me volvieran a este cuarto, lo reconocería por el olor. Yo conozco los cuartos por el olor. El año pasado Ada me había sentado en sus piernas. Estaba quedándome verdaderamente dormido cuando sentí el olor» (pp. 64-65). Isabel's involuntary memory also starts to function as a result of the train whistle: «Oigo pitar el tren en la última vuelta. 'Son las dos y media,' pienso; y no puedo sortear la idea de que a esta hora todo Macondo está pendiente de lo que hacemos en esta casa. Pienso en la señora Rebeca» (p. 19). In chapter ten, the appearance of the room reminds the Colonel of his first visit to the same room: «Es la segunda vez que vengo a este cuarto. La primera, hace diez años, las cosas estaban en el mismo orden. Es como si él no hubiera vuelto a tocar nada desde entonces, o como si desde esa remota madrugada en que se vino a vivir con Meme no hubiera vuelto a ocuparse de su vida. Como si hubiera sido ayer cuando El Cachorro y yo vinimos a concertar la paz entre este hombre y las autoridades» (p. 109). In the first chapter, García Márquez establishes the framework for the memory processes which will function uninterruptedly throughout the rest of the novel. By introducing narrators who represent three different generations, he creates a prismatic, multiple effect. The boy can remember only the events of the most recent past. Isabel, who is almost thirty, can recall a more distant past. The Colonel, because of his direct involvement in the doctor's and Macondo's past, covers the greatest time span. The narrators engage in what Mircea Eliade calls historical memory, which involves the «meticulous and exhaustive recollecting of personal and historical events.» [12] They initiate their recreation of the past in the present, and García Márquez inverts the normal temporal sequence so that the novel begins at the end. *H* opens with the effects of the events (the doctor's suicide and Macondo's present moribund state), and the narrators will supposedly reveal their causes by returning through memory to the beginning (the doctor's arrival and Macondo's founding). [13] To create this time in reverse, García Márquez employs a series of flashbacks which combine to form the temporal montage of the novel. [14] García Márquez chooses the technique of soliloquy in order to transmit the content of the three narrators' historical memories. The soliloquy, «although it is spoken *solus*, nevertheless is represented with the assumption of a formal and immediate audience,» and its purpose is «to communicate emotions and ideas which are related to a plot and action.» [15] Each narrator speaks alone, and each chapter division is an individual unit which exposes ideas and emotions linked to either the history of Macondo or the doctor's past. Lastly, each soliloquy presupposes the presence of an immediate audience which, in this case, is the reader. [16] Free association unifies the network of images which «are not· serially, progressively, and uniformly ordered but are always inextricably and dynamically associated and mixed up with each other.»[17] Memory possesses its own particular causality which may appear confusing and illogical to another person, but it coheres for the person remembering.

The three narrators' memories merge to create a chronological sequence as they slowly reconstruct the fragments of Macondo's and the doctor's past. Isabel and the Colonel offer the widest use of free association, while the young boy's principal contribution is to describe what is happening in the present. When the Colonel looks at the doctor's old newspapers which have not been opened, he associates them with a past event: «Y los más antiguos: *Octubre de 1919.* Pienso: *Hace nueve años, uno después de pronunciada la sentencia, que no abría los periódicos. Había renunciado desde entonces a lo último que lo vinculaba a su tierra y a su gente»* (p. 28). Isabel combines three different events:«Cuando la enfermedad de papá, *hace tres años*, el doctor no había salido de esta esquina una sola vez, *después de la noche* en que le negó su asistencia a los heridos lo mismo que *seis años antes* se la había negado a la mujer que *dos días después* sería su concubina» (p. 33, italics mine). A multitude of different associations comes into play when she remembers the appearance of her sick father that she links to *El Cachorro*'s funeral:

> Yo lo recuerdo al quinto día de postración, disminuido entre las sábanas; recuerdo su cuerpo diezmado, como el cuerpo de *El Cachorro* que el año anterior había sido conducido al cementerio por todos los habitantes de Macondo, en una apretada y conmovida procesión floral. Dentro del ataúd, su majestuosidad tenía el mismo fondo de irremediable y desconsolado abandono que yo veía en el rostro de mi padre en esos días en que la alcoba se llenó de su voz y habló de aquel extraño militar que en la guerra del 85 apareció una noche en el campamento del coronel Aureliano Buendía, con el sombrero y las botas adornadas con pieles y dientes y uñas de tigre (p. 120).

The associations multiply until the most distant past is reached, and the resulting temporal pattern disrupts chronology. The Colonel's second visit to the doctor's room recalls his first one which in turn is associated with the banana company: «Como si hubiera sido ayer cuando *El Cachorro* y yo vinimos a concertar la paz entre este hombre y las autoridades. Para entonces, la compañía bananera había acabado de exprimirnos, y se había ido de Macondo» (pp. 109-110).

Although the reader can reconstruct a more precise chronology from the fragments, they must be gleaned from the network of associations.

Memory plays a key role in the creation of myth in *H*. Macondo's and the doctor's pasts are situated along the vertical time axis which constantly cuts through the horizontal, linear time of the half-hour. Memory transfers past events from chronological time to the continuous present, and all the events, despite their different stages of development, occupy the same temporal frame. The doctor's story is fully developed, whereas Macondo's founding is only partially revealed. The banana company, the civil war and Colonel Aureliano Buendía are briefly mentioned. Past, present and future merge to from a timeless domain in which every past event associated with Macondo will eventually be more fully exposed. [18] The doctor's story represents only one event which has occurred in the mythical place of Macondo. Macondo, liberated from the bonds of historical time, can be located in the timeless realm of myth.

Isabel's and the Colonel's soliloquies reveal the strong presence of circular time. Their viewpoints describe a world in which nothing changes, whose individual and collective histories no longer advance or retrogress, and whose circular path points to the eternal return of the same. They view human existence in fatalistic terms, and although fatalism cannot be automatically equated with cyclical time, a negative, pessimistic outlook is generally attributed to it. [19] Isabel considers her presence in the room with the doctor's body an ineluctable evolution of history beyond her control: «Pero algo me indicaba que era impotente ante el curso que iban tomando los acontecimientos. No era yo quien disponía las cosas en mi hogar, sino otra fuerza misteriosa, que ordenaba el curso de nuestra existencia y de la cual no éramos otra cosa que un dócil e insignificante instrumento. Todo parecía obedecer entonces al natural y eslabonado cumplimiento de una profecía» (p. 99). Everything seems written in some indelible ink which man cannot alter: «Ahora no, porque otro capítulo de la fatalidad había empezado a cumplirse desde hacía tres meses» (p. 101). History becomes a series of events that man simply experiences and cannot direct: «*Desde cuando el doctor abandonó nuestra casa, yo estaba convencido de que nuestros actos eran ordenados por una voluntad superior contra la cual no habríamos podido rebelarnos, así lo hubiéramos procurado con todas nuestras fuerzas o así hubiéramos asumido la actitud estéril de Adelaida que se ha encerrado a rezar. Pero todo eso parecía dispuesto, ordenado para encauzar hechos que, paso a paso, nos conducirían fatalmente a este miércoles*» (pp. 121-22).

These karmic views of man oppose Sartre's existentialist formula according to which man's existence precedes his essence. In *H*, man's existence becomes «esa amarga materia de fatalidad» (p. 122) which has destroyed Macondo and directs the lives of all the characters. Man experiences his existence in an essentially passive manner, which Vargas Llosa links to the fatalistic vision of history: «El hombre es una esencia anterior a su existencia, que la praxis no puede en ningún caso cambiar. El destino individual y el colectivo, la historia de un hombre y la de la comunidad, son meras manifestaciones de 'esencias' eternas e inmutables. La voluntad humana no puede alterar lo que existe como potencialidad fatídica en cada hombre o pueblo desde antes de su nacimiento.»[20] Cyclical time divests man of his ability to act and create history, and he can only adapt himself to the rhythm of the eternal cycle of birth, growth, decline and death. The rest of his existence is nothing but repetition, the eternal return of the same, and his acts change nothing.

Despite these pessimistic pronouncements, the cyclical theory of time contributes to the creation of myth in *H*. Cyclical time, which often appears in conjunction with myth, helps García Márquez forge a myth which will, in the words of Hans Meyerhoff, «suggest a timeless perspective of looking upon the human situation; and to convey a sense of continuity and identification with mankind in general.»[21] With Macondo situated in a timeless scheme, it can be an «ever present, a constant reminder of the eternal return of the same.»[22] Vargas Llosa describes circular time in *H* as «algo circular: cada minuto contiene a los otros, el final está en el principio y viceversa.»[23] Circular time provides a context in which Macondo can exist without beginning or end, and the myth of Macondo is converted into a circular series of events which can appear and disappear at different intervals. The basic myth of Macondo remains constant, but with each completion of the circular path of time, its components can be restructured.

· *H*'s time categories establish the timelessness in which the myth of Macondo can exist. The continuous present places Macondo and the doctor's story in a framework beyond chronological time. The doctor's story, although overshadowing Macondo, represents only one event which takes place there. Memory reveals Macondo through the subjective time of the three narrators, and timelessness is achieved as each narrator removes the events from chronological time and places them in a mythical scheme. Circular time transforms Macondo into a mythical place where everything can recommence. Although this Macondo has a particular historicity, it constitutes García Márquez' first version of a mythical place in which he can situate other mythical events.

NOTES

1. Two important studies devoted to *La hojarasca* were published before the appearance of *Cien años de soledad* in 1967: Pedro Lastra, «La tragedia como fundamento estructural de *La hojarasca*,» *Anales de la Universidad de Chile,* Año CXXIV, No. 140, (octubre-diciembre de 1966), pp. 168-186 and Juan Loveluck, «Gabriel García Márquez, narrador colombiano,» *Duquesne Hispanic Review,* No. 3, (1966), pp. 135-54. Both of these studies also appear in: *Nueve asedios a García Márquez* (Santiago de Chile: Editorial Universitaria, S.A., 1971), pp. 38-51 and 52-73 respectively. Important studies published after the appearance of *Cien años de soledad* include: Graciela Maturo, «El sentido religioso de *La hojarasca* de Gabriel García Márquez,» *Eco,* Tomo XXIV Nos. 140-142, (enero-febrero, 1972), pp. 217-235. This same study also appears in: Graciela Maturo, *Claves simbólicas de García Márquez* (Buenos Aires: Fernando García Cambiero, 1972), pp. 77-90. The second study is: Mario Vargas Llosa, *García Márquez: historia de un deicidio* (Barcelona: Barral Editores, 1971), pp. 243-291. Another study of note is: Franz García de Paredes, «Aproximación a García Márquez: *La hojarasca,*» Diss. Florida State, 1972.

This chapter appeared in slightly different form as: «García Márquez' *La hojarasca:* Paradigm of Time and Search for Myth,» *Hispania,* Vol. 59, No. 4 (December, 1976), pp. 810-19.

2. Gabriel García Márquez—Mario Vargas Llosa, *La novela en América Latina: diálogo*(Lima: Carlos Milla Batres—Ediciones Universidad Nacional de Ingeniería, 1971), p. 47.

3. Mario Vargas Llosa, *García Márquez: historia de un deicidio* (Barcelona: Barral Editores, 1971), p. 246.

4. Gabriel García Márquez, *La hojarasca* (Buenos Aires: Editorial Sudamericana, 1969). Isabel notes the hour on pages 20, 62, 64, and 127 as does her son on page 132. All successive quotes will be taken from this edition and page numbers will be indicated in parentheses.

5. Juan Loveluck, «Gabriel García Márquez: narrador colombiano,» *Nueve asedios a García Márquez* (Santiago: Editorial Universitaria, S.A., 1971) pp. 67-8.

6. Juan Loveluck, p. 68.

7. *La hojarasca* is divided into eleven chapters. These chapters are further subdivided into twenty-eight individual frames that form a structure resembling the process of temporal montage. Robert Humphrey, *Stream of Consciousness in the Modern Novel* (Berkeley: University of California Press, 1972), p. 49, defines montage as a class of devices «which are used to show the interrelation or association of ideas, such as a rapid succession of images or the superimposition of image on image or the surrounding of a focal image by related ones. It is essentially a method to show composite or diverse views of one subject—in short, to show multiplicity.» In *La hojarasca,* temporal mon-

tage (as opposed to spatial) plays the dominant role in the total structure. In temporal montage, a character does not move, but his mind or consciousness is free to roam over a wide temporal spectrum. The three narrators in *La hojarasca* are stationary while they project their minds into the past.

8. Pedro Lastra, «La tragedia como fundamento estructural de *La hojarasca*,» in: *Sobre García Márquez*, ed. Pedro Simón Martínez (Montevideo: Biblioteca de Marcha, 1971), p. 79.

9. Roger Shattuck, *Marcel Proust* (New York: The Viking Press, 1974), p. 143.

10. *Ibid.*, p. 143.

11. Shiv K. Kumar, *Bergson and the Stream of Consciousness Novel* (New York: New York University Press, 1963), p. 28.

12. Mircea Eliade, *Myth and Reality,* trans. Willard R. Trask (New York: Harper & Row, Publishers, 1963), p. 89.

13. Vargas Llosa defines García Márquez' narrative technique in *La hojarasca* in the following manner: «...*narrar por omisión o mediante omisiones significativas, en silenciar temporal o definitivamente ciertos datos de la historia para dar más relieve o fuerza narrativa a esos mismos datos que han sido momentánea o totalmente suprimidos.*» *(García Márquez: historia de un deicidio,* p. 279). Certain gaps concerning the doctor's and Macondo's past have been created so that the reader is left with a series of questions at the end of the novel.

14. García Márquez is well acquainted with film techniques. He studied at the Centro Sperimentale de Cinematografia in Rome while he was a reporter in Europe for the Colombian newspaper, *El Espectador.*

15. Robert Humphrey, pp. 35-6.

16. The Colonel speaks in 13 soliloquies, Isabel in 10 and her son in 6. The Colonel is also the author of the unsigned prologue dated «Macondo, 1909.» The prologue represents a compact history of certain events that could only have been written by someone who directly participated in them.

17. Hans Meyerhoff, *Time in Literature* (Berkeley: Unviersity of California Press, 1968), p. 24.

18. If, according to Lévi-Strauss, the specific pattern of myth explains the past, present as well as the future, this statement is a little more problematic in relation to *La hojarasca*. In terms of narration in the novel, «el pasado, el presente y el futuro coexisten como un todo, más no con la misma prominencia, ni como categorías similares.» (Franz García de Paredes, p. 44). In terms of the myth of Macondo, the past is explained by a series of events whose causes are not fully revealed. The myth only partially explains the present in *La hojarasca* which is submerged by the weight of the past. The future, in relation to the action in the novel, does not exist because «cuando se abre la posibilidad de un futuro, es decir, cuando se inicia la procesion funeral, la novela se termina. El futuro de los acontecimientos queda en suspenso y no se nos revela.» (Franz García de Paredes, p. 45). The future, in relation to the myth of Macondo, is an abbreviated form and functions as an apocalyptic vision: «...y allí estará esta tarde, cuando regresemos

del entierro, si es que entonces no ha pasado todavía ese viento final que barrerá a Macondo, sus dormitorios llenos de lagartos y su gente taciturna, devastada por los recuerdos.» *(La hojarasca,* p. 129). This future prediction of an apocalyptic end for Macondo can also be found at the end of «Los funerales de la Mamá Grande» (p. 147) and at the end of *Cien años de soledad* (p. 351). The past and present of Macondo hint at such an end, but this cannot be firmly established. The myth of Macondo in *La hojarasca* does not completely explain the past, the present and the future. This is due to the fact that the past contains many gaps that reduce its explanatory function.

19. «The timeless law of the eternal return is indifferent to the value of the temporal manifestations of this law. Time may be, and will always be, a source of both good and evil. In fact, to accept this principle meant for Nietzsche to take a position 'beyond good and evil.' This value-neutrality, however, is usually felt by most people to contain a negative, pessimistic outlook simply because *good* (as well as evil) is ruled out by the eternal cycles.» (Hans Meyerhoff, pp. 79-80).

20. Vargas Llosa, pp. 270-271.

21. Meyerhoff, p. 80.

22. *Ibid.,* p. 80.

23. Vargas Llosa, p. 274.

THE MYTHICAL TRANSITION:
«LOS FUNERALES DE LA MAMA GRANDE»

CHAPTER 2

In *FMG,* García Márquez succeeds in making the final transition from the somewhat fragmented, experimental nature of the previous works to the cohesive unity of *CAS.* Carmen Arnau has noted this point: «*Los funerales de la Mamá Grande* es el último cuento y el que da título al libro. Tanto el lenguaje como el tono anuncian *Cien años de soledad;* hay incluso muchas afinidades temáticas.»[1] Two principal elements contribute to the creation of myth in *FMG:* (1) the use of the *voz callejera* viewpoint; and (2) the *bricolage* construction of the short story.

Vargas Llosa defines the *voz callejera* in the following way:

> La perspectiva en la cual se ha instalado el narrador es la de la leyenda y el mito, ese nivel de lo real que tiende a hinchar, a exagerar los datos de lo real objetivo. Es esa voz callejera, la voz de la hipérbole y de la invención, la que nos cuenta esta historia. Todo el relato mantiene ese carácter de pregón, de cosa dicha en medio de la calle y a gritos, para que no la opaquen los otros transeúntes. El narrador ha hecho suya la perspectiva de la gente que, en la calle, chismea, murmura, se apodera de los hechos real objetivos y los manipula con la fantasía, aumentándolos, coloreándolos, mundándolos en mito y leyenda. Lo que se nos va a contar no es la verdad histórica, lo que ocurrió, sino aquello en que la fantasía y el chisme populares convirtieron lo ocurrido, el mito en que el suceso histórico quedó transformado.[2]

The *voz callejera* is opposed to history, which, as Warner Berthoff states, «is reserved for that species of narrative in which we try to describe something that has happened according to the discoverable testimony about it and by means of certifiable techniques for gathering and identifying such testimony.»[3] Historical narration is chronological and descriptive, and aspires to objectivity in its presentation of past events. History is primarily a written, composed mode of narration designed to «reveal a preexistent order of actuality.»[4] The *voz callejera* involves the oral interpretation of events by a storyteller, who arranges them as he tells his story.

The oral aspect of the *voz callejera* links it closely to myth and mythical narration. Robert Kellogg and Robert Scholes define myth as «a traditional plot which can be transmitted.»[5] Warner Berthoff states that myth means «simply the thing said—the word, saying, or speech, but also (in the modality of narrative) the basic sequence of utterance required to set out the indispensable agents and occurrences of the story.»[6] Berthoff clearly distinguishes between mythical and historical narration: «Myths are *told,* and we do not know their particular origin. Histories are reasembled. That is, we do not know myth as a making, only as a telling. Myths, in fact, are not to be known or encountered directly but only through the performance of tellers, only, that is, in fictive versions, retellings.»[7] Claude Lévi-Strauss also stresses the oral nature of myth: «There is a very good reason why myth cannot simply be treated as language if its specific problems are to be solved; myth *is* language: to be known, myth has to be told; it is a part of human speech.»[8] Given the close relationship between the *voz callejera* and mythical narration, García Márquez develops a narrative mode fundamentally different from history. Although *FMG* is a written text, it becomes a transcription of this mythical narrative. The *voz callejera* also resembles myth because the narrator remains anonymous. In *FMG,* García Márquez establishes both the oral aspect of mythical narration and the anonymity of the narrator.

García Márquez omits the historical event which has already transpired: «Ahora que la nación sacudida en sus entrañas ha recobrado el equilibrio...»[9] The repetition of «ahora que» emphasizes that he will recreate what has already taken place. Although it is not a question of reproducing the timeless pattern of an ancient myth, García Márquez' use of the *voz callejera* recreates a myth whose structure differs radically from the chronology of history. That myth, of course, is the myth of Macondo. He clearly establishes his mythical, oral stance at the beginning: «...ahora es la hora de recostar un taburete a la puerta de la calle y empezar a contar desde el principio los pormenores de esta conmoción nacional, antes de que tengan tiempo de llegar los historiadores» (p. 127). The narrator resembles the ancient storyteller who gathers around him a group of younger people to whom he will impart his version of a myth. The storyteller proceeds to give a mythical account of a historical event which he summarizes on the first page of the story (p. 127). García Márquez' storyteller also intervenes at several other points in the story: «...además de los que se enumeran al principio de esta crónica, y muchos otros...» (p. 144); «...y todas las que se omiten por no hacer interminables estas crónicas» (p. 145); «Sólo faltaba entonces que alguien recostara un taburete en la puerta para contar esta historia...» (p. 147). These quotations constitute what Harald Weinrich calls «recurrent textual signals» of mythical narration which indicate the narrative sequence.[10] The word «crónica» implies a certain order, but García Márquez' «crónica» is not objective. Mythologists generally agree that myth recounts a series of events, but they disagree over their particular order. García Márquez' narrative will consist of a series of events, but each new storyteller will modify its order. The last indication of the storyteller's presence (p. 147) simultaneously represents a conclusion of the story and another narrative beginning. The new storyteller will retain the basic components of the myth of Macondo, but he will rearrange them in order to produce a new version. The structure of *FMG* also contributes to the creation of myth.

Claude Lévi-Strauss' concept of *bricolage* is central to understanding *FMG*'s mythical structure. Warner Berthoff clearly defines *bricolage* which Lévi-Strauss develops in *The Savage Mind:*

> To distinguish the special character of mythical thought from propositional or ideological thinking, Lévi-Strauss draws an amusing contrast between two kinds of workmen, the engineer and the *bricoleur* (a term which defies translation: it combines a sense of someone who does odd jobs in an unsystematic, pottering way and someone who introduces antic and extraneous elements into sports and games). The engineer defines a project, assembles the precise equipment or «instrumental set» needed for it, and carries it through in the most efficient way. The *bricoleur,* occupying himself with a comparable project, is not comparably direct in his treatment of it but positively devious and refractory. He uses not a limited set of instruments appropriate to that one job but everything he has at hand.

The *bricoleur's* performance is as much ceremonial as practical, and it includes a built-in principle of expansion that rejects shortcuts. The *bricoleur* does perform real work. But he does it the long way around, as in a game the object of which is not to win but to try out all known strokes and engage to their own satisfaction all available personnel. So with any one task the *bricoleur* first «interrogates all the heteroclite objects of which his treasury is composed to discover what each of them could 'signify,'» thus contributing to the definition of a new set that differs from a purely instrumental one by the principle according to which its parts are disposed and by the refusal to exclude anything for reasons of efficiency.[11]

G. S. Kirk, comparing the *bricoleur* to a mythmaker, states that the mythmaker «allows the structure of his mind, already reproduced in the structure of society, to find reflexion in the structure or interrelationships of the symbols that he puts together in a myth. The value of the symbols themselves is indifferent; what matters is the relation they bear to each other. It is in this way that he works like a handyman, creating a structure out of what comes to hand.»[12] These explanations stress the close relationship between the *bricoleur* and the storyteller, for both use the elements they have at hand to create a structure whose final arrangement cannot be envisioned at the outset. The storyteller's primary tool is narration, and he employs it to rearrange the basic constituents of the myth of Macondo into a new pattern which will have a *bricolage* structure. Lévi-Strauss' distinction between the creative acts in works of art and myth further illustrates this idea: «In the case of works of art, the starting point is a set of one or more objects and one or more events which aesthetic creation unifies by revealing a common structure. Myths travel the same road but start from the other end. They use a structure to produce what is itself an object consisting of a set of events (for all myths tell a story). Art thus proceeds from a set (object + event) to the *discovery* of its structure. Myth starts from a structure by means of which it *constructs* a set (object + event).»[13] The historian, for example, proceeds from a set (a series of events) in order to create a chronological structure. The storyteller, like myth, starts from a structure (i.e., the myth of Macondo) and constructs a set (another version of the myth of Macondo).

In *FMG,* the *bricoleur*-storyteller places his story in a mythical context. Macondo is again the setting for *FMG:* «Esta es, incrédulos del mundo entero, la verídica historia de la Mamá Grande, soberana absoluta del reino de Macondo» (p. 127). The storyteller's announcement of what he is going to recount constitutes one of the elements of mythical narration which Harald Weinrich calls «metalinguistic signals»; that is, «the announcement by the narrator that he is going to narrate a myth.»[14] Macondo is seen in relation to other geographical places that are enumerated at various points:

> los gaiteros de San Jacinto, los contrabandistas de la Guajira, los arroceros del Sinú, las prostitutas de Guacamayal, los hechiceros de la Sierpe y los bananeros de Aracataca. Allí estaban las lavanderas del San Jorge, los pescadores de perla del Cabo de Vela, los atarrayeros de Ciénaga, los camaroneros de Tasajera, los brujos de la Mojana, los salineros de Manaure, los acordeoneros de Valledupar, los chalanes de Ayapel, los papayeros de San Pelayo, los mamadores de gallo de La Cueva, los improvisadores de las Sabanas de Bolívar, los camajanes de Rebolo, los bogas del Magdalena, los tinterillos de Mompox. (pp. 127, 144)

Enumeration gives Macondo a sort of geographical reality, but García Márquez never pinpoints its location. Although enumeration is not particular to mythical narration, the storyteller uses it to expand Macondo's boundaries. Not only does he use the actual names of Colombian towns, but he also adds a number of imaginary places and people to enlarge Macondo's geographical situation.[15] Macondo thus becomes an umbilical cord for this geographical region because everyone comes there to attend the funeral. If Macondo is a geographical macrocosm, it is also a microcosm whose boundaries are as finite as Mamá Grande's real empire: «Reducido a sus proporciones reales, el patrimonio físico se reducía a tres encomiendas adjudicadas por Cédula Real durante la Colonia, y que con el transcurso del tiempo, en virtud de intricados matrimonios de conveniencia, se habían acumulado bajo el dominio de la Mamá Grande. En ese territorio ocioso, sin límites definidos, que abarcaba cinco municipios y en el cual no se sembró nunca un solo grano por cuenta de los propietarios, vivían a título de arrendatarias 352 familias» (pp. 134-35). Macondo's reduced position no longer makes it the crossroads of the world. This seemingly contradictory image of a Macondo whose mythical proportions are suddenly reduced reveals the storyteller's *bricolage* technique of composing his story. Since he is recounting a version of the myth of Macondo, he can present a different version. Macondo the town differs from the myth of Macondo because it makes up one of the gross constituents that together form the myth of Macondo.

If Macondo itself has decreased in size, its mythico-geographical context has grown considerably. Its spatial context extends to the «sombrío promontorio del Castelsantangello en el horizonte del Tíber» (p. 142). From Rome the Supreme Pontiff can take his «larga góndola negra, rumbo a los fantásticos y remotos funerales de la Mamá Grande» (p. 142), and in one night, he can arrive in Macondo. Macondo's spatial context represents a secondary element that the storyteller has included in his version, and its boundaries fluctuate substantially between *H* and *CAS*. The addition of a number of fantastic details also expands Macondo's mythical context. Stylistically, the storyteller employs exaggeration so that «todos los componentes de la realidad ficticia sufren cambios cuantitativos. Aumentan, se alargan en el tiempo y se extienden en el espacio, sus propiedades se proyectan a un nivel de excepcionalidad, se potencian hasta un límite extremo.»[16] The storyteller thus converts Macondo into a paradigm consistent with his narrative method.

García Márquez' storyteller employs a set of heteroclite elements (Macondo, all the other geographical places mentioned, Rome, the Vatican and Castelsantangello) to create a mythical realm of which Macondo is the center. By combining apparently unrelated objects, he is able to create a mythical framework in which Macondo is simultaneously a microcosmic entity and a macrocosmic one by association with the other places. This double view of Macondo demonstrates the storyteller's *bricolage* technique of arranging the elements of his story according to their relational possibilities. Macondo can present this dual image because it is the direct result of the combination of the elements the storyteller has at his disposal.

Macondo also undergoes a temporal protraction. In *H,* people fleeing the civil wars of the past century settled in Macondo whereas in *FMG,* it is at least three hundred years old: «Durante el presente siglo, la Mamá Grande había sido el centro de gravedad de Macondo, como sus hermanos, sus padres y los padres de sus padres lo fueron en el pasado, en una hegemonía que colmaba dos siglos» (p. 129). Macondo's origin is indicated by another event: «...el patrimonio físico se reducía a tres encomiendas adjudicadas por Cédula Real durante la Colonia...» (pp. 134-135). The various phases of Mamá Grande's past are revealed in her age: «...en función de dominio durante 92 años...» (p. 127); «Pero ella confiaba en que viviría más de 100 años...» (p. 130); and «La Mamá Grande, que hasta los cincuenta años...» (p. 133). These numbers constitute a «historical account» of her life, but the storyteller dissociates them from any years. In *H*, the reader can still reconstruct Macondo's chronological history because of the presence of certain dates. In *FMG*, García Márquez has omitted all years but one, a technique which he will use again in *CAS*. As Lévi-Strauss explains, myth exhibits a «double structure altogether historical and ahistorical *[and]* always refers to events alleged to have taken place long ago.»[17] Myth can contain temporal references, but its events are not chronologically arranged by using years. García Márquez recognizes this duality in myth, and by eliminating years, the storyteller is free to arrange the other temporal references.

The temporal context also protracts or contracts with the flow of the mythical narration. At various points the storyteller designates precisely when certain events occurred:

«La Mamá Grande...murió en olor de santidad un martes del setiembre pasado... (p. 127).

Hace catorce semanas...la Mamá Grande ordenó que la sentaran en su viejo mecedor de bejuco para expresar su última voluntad (p. 128).

Sólo en abril de este año comprendió la Mamá Grande... (p. 130).

En la primera semana de dolores el médico de la familia... (p. 130).

y durante tres semanas embadurnó a la moribunda por dentro y por afuera... (p. 131).

Aquella tradición se había interrumpido, en parte por los duelos sucesivos de la familia, y en parte por la incertidumbre política de los últimos tiempos (p. 132).

Los habitantes de la capital remota y sombría vieron esa tarde... (p. 137).

Durante muchos años la Mamá Grande había garantizado la paz... (p. 139).

Así vivió semanas interminables y meses alargados por la expectativa... (pp. 143-44).

El gran día era venido (p. 144).

The storyteller, like the *bricoleur* who constructs structured sets from the «fossilized evidence of history of an individual or a society,» presents precise oddments of events that in no way constitute chronological history.[18] They belong to the heterogeneous collection of elements which the storyteller is in the process of arranging.

The allusions to the civil wars also belong to the storyteller's heterogeneous repertory. First, he alludes to the civil wars of 1875 which have supposedly ended: «...que en la guerra de 1875 *[*Mamá Grande's grandmother*]* se enfrentó a una patrulla del coronel Aureliano Buendía, atrincherada en la cocina de la hacienda» (p. 130). But it is still possible that the civil wars continue: «Sólo en abril de este año comprendió la Mamá Grande que Dios no le concedería el privilegio de liquidar personalmente, en franca refriega, a una horda de masones federalistas» (p. 130). The problem is further complicated by another reference to Colonel Aureliano Buendía: «Bajo los almendros polvorientos donde la primera semana del siglo acamparon las legiones del coronel Aureliano Buendía...» (p. 131). Finally, the Colonel's veterans have come to the funeral: «Hasta los veteranos del coronel Aureliano Buendía...vinieron a los funerales, para solicitar del presidente de la república el pago de las pensiones de guerra que esperaban desde hacía sesenta años» (p. 144). This last allusion would imply that the civil wars had ended long ago.[19] The storyteller gives specific temporal references (including the year 1875), but they do not follow a chronological sequence. He is therefore able to incorporate them into his *bricolage* construction to create an ahistorical presentation of the civil wars.

This ahistorical arrangement of the myth of Macondo is dominated by the figure of Mamá Grande. The question arises whether Mamá Grande is a gross constituent of the overall myth of Macondo or a major component of this particular version. As a gross constituent, Mamá Grande would have to appear in all the variants of the myth of Macondo. On the one hand, she is a prototype of the women in the myth of Macondo who are undoubtedly a gross constituent. On the other hand, she is reduced to one sentence in *CAS.*[20] Mamá Grande, like the French doctor in *H,* forms a core element in one variant of the myth of Macondo. Mamá Grande is a gross constituent in the sense that women are common to all versions of the myth of Macondo, but she herself dominates only one version.

As the absolute ruler, Mamá Grande assures the cohesiveness of her empire by a series of endogamic relationships:

> La rigidez matriarcal de la Mamá Grande había cercado su fortuna y su apellido con una alambrada sacramental, dentro del cual los tíos se casaban con las hijas de las sobrinas, y los primos con las tías, y los hermanos con las cuñadas, hasta formar una intricada maraña de consanguinidad que convirtió la procreación en un círculo vicioso. Al margen de la familia oficial, y en ejercicio del derecho de pernada los varones habían fecundado hatos, veredas y caseríos con toda una descendencia bastarda, que circulaba entre la servidumbre sin apellidos a título de ahijadas, dependientes, favoritos y protegidos de la Mamá Grande (p. 129).

Mamá Grande, like the gods of antiquity who frequently engendered offspring through incestuous relationships, insures the continuation of her own essence by having members of her own family unite. Everything has been enlarged and exaggerated in relation to Mamá Grande. When she assumed the role of absolute ruler of Macondo after her father's death, there were two hundred yards of matting which were laid down from the manorial house to the high altar, and she installed herself on the throne invested with her new and radiant dignity. No one lent much credence to the idea that she was a mere mortal. The excess of her power and her physical appearance affected those around her. The Padre Antonio Isabel needed ten men to take him up to Big Mamá's bedroom. Her death caused a national commotion. Its prodigious repercussions extended all the way to Rome. It assembles «el presidente de la república y sus ministros y todos aquellos que representaron al poder público y a las potencias sobrenaturales en la más espléndida ocasión funeraria que registren los anales históricos» (p. 127). News of her death first reached the capital of the country, then spread to the highest ranks of the world's religious authorities. Her death brought people from everywhere to Macondo. Also included in this heterogeneous conglomeration was the Supreme Pontiff.

The events and characters of a myth often seem hyperbolized to our modern, logic-oriented minds. One primary function of myth is to speak of highly significant subjects in a narrative sequence, but our modern age has dissociated these important subjects from narrative style. García Márquez has revitalized this primary function of myth in *FMG*. Exaggeration, instead of being used to ridicule, aids the storyteller in speaking narratively about an important subject belonging to the myth of Macondo. Myth, as Warner Berthoff states, becomes a way of bringing «the multiplicity of things that are known about, and the speech terms by which they are known, into an order in which they will continue to exist and be serviceable.»[21] This order is the narrative that other storytellers can recreate.

García Marquez is still searching for the final form which the mythical Macondo will take, and he will continue to restructure its basic elements to recreate it in a different setting. The end of the story also signals the demise of this particular Macondo which the storyteller has constructed: «...que mañana miércoles vendrán los barrenderos y barrerán la basura de sus funerales, por todos los siglos de los siglos» (p. 147). This last sentence also reveals the presence of the storyteller who has concluded his story. In *FMG,* García Márquez succeeds in restoring to myth its orality, whereas in his previous novels and short stories, as Vargas Llosa points out, «la escritura ambicionaba la transparencia: precisa, discreta, se soldaba al objeto para mostrarlo imparcialmente, desaparecía en él. La palabra *decía* el mundo ficticio, era invisible, describía sin opinar, exponía sin interferir.»[22] García Márquez recognized the inadequacy of this style in creating the myth of Macondo, and introduced two important innovations in *FMG* which aid substantially in the creation of myth: the *voz callejera* and the *bricolage* construction of his story. Vargas Llosa states that the *voz callejera* corresponds to the point of view of the inhabitants of Macondo, but in terms of the myth of Macondo, it is more appropriately the storyteller's viewpoint which is conveying this version of the myth of Macondo. The *voz callejera* transfers the story from a historical to an oral perspective which is the basic point of view of myth. It also allows the storyteller to incorporate certain stylistic techniques, such as exaggeration and enumeration, into his oral viewpoint. *FMG*'s *bricolage* construction flows from the *voz callejera* viewpoint. Since the storyteller is free to compose his narrative of Mamá Grande's funeral, its final form, as in the case of the *bricoleur,* will depend on the use he makes of all the elements he has at hand. His project is to tell a story, but it has no predetermined form.

García Márquez' deletion of dates liberates his storyteller from historical chronology. In *H,* García Márquez adumbrated the myth of Macondo, but the town of Macondo still has a history. The myth of Macondo in *H* does not fully materialize because the events described are still considered historical. In *FMG,* García Márquez places the events in a mythical perspective, in which Macondo as a mythical place can flourish. García Márquez has created the town of Macondo in order to engender the myth of Macondo, and this myth embraces a much wider gamut of material. García Márquez, who is the storyteller, necessarily reflects the structure and values of Latin

America in his myth. In *CAS*, he perfects his techniques and vision, but *FMG* represents freedom and discovery: freedom to create the myth of Macondo and discovery of the techniques to achieve it.

NOTES

1. Carmen Arnau, *El mundo mítico de Gabriel García Márquez* (Barcelona: Ediciones Península, 1971), p. 34.

This chapter first appeared as: «The Creation of Myth in García Márquez' *Los funerales de la Mamá Grande*,» *Hispania*, Vol. 61, No. 1 (March, 1978), pp. 14-23.

2. Mario Vargas Llosa, *García Márquez: historia de un deicidio* (Barcelona: Barral Editores, 1971), pp. 400-01.

3. Warner Berthoff, *Fictions and Events: Essays in Criticism and Literary History* (New York: E. P. Dutton & Co., Inc., 1971), p. 38.

4. *Ibid.*, p. 40.

5. Robert Scholes and Robert Kellogg, *The Nature of Narrative* (New York: Oxford Unviersity Press, 1966), p. 12.

6. Berthoff, pp. 43-44.

7. *Ibid.*, p. 44.

8. Claude Lévi-Strauss, *Structural Anthropology*, trans. Claire Jacobson and Brooke Grundfest Schoepf (Garden City, New York: Doubleday & Company, Inc., 1967), p. 205.

9. Gabriel García Márquez, *Los funerales de la Mamá Grande* (Buenos Aires: Editorial Sudamericana, 1969), p. 127. All successive quotes will come from this edition and page numbers will be given in parentheses.

10. Harald Weinrich, «Structures narratives du mythe,» *Poétique*, I (1970), p. 27. Translations are mine.

11. Berthoff, pp. 48-49.

12. G. S. Kirk, *Myth, its Meaning and Functions in Ancient and Other Cultures* (London: The Cambridge University Press, 1970), pp. 81-82.

13. Claude Lévi-Strauss, *The Savage Mind* (Chicago: The University of Chicago Press, 1970), p. 26.

14. Harald Weinrich, p. 27.

15. Real geographical names mentioned in *FMG* include San Jacinto, la Guajira (department), Aracataca, Cabo de la Vela, Ciénaga, Valledupar, Manuare, Bolívar (department), Magdalena (department) and Mompox (Mompós on map), pp. 127 and 144.

16. Vargas Llosa, pp. 402-03.

17. Lévi-Strauss, *Structural Anthropology*, p. 205.

18. Lévi-Strauss, *The Savage Mind*, p. 22.

19. An excellent discussion of this point can be found in Vargas Llosa, pp. 416-17.

20. Gabriel García Márquez, *Cien años de soledad*, (Buenos Aires: Editorial Sudamericana, 1967), p. 69. All other quotes will be taken from this edition and page numbers will be given in parentheses.)

21. Berthoff, P. 50.

22. Vargas Llosa, p. 411.

THE *BRICOLAGE* AND MYTHICAL STRUCTURE OF *CIEN AÑOS DE SOLEDAD*

CHAPTER 3

Although much critical discussion has been devoted to the structure of *CAS,* García Márquez has not provided any detailed explanations. In an interview in 1970, González Bermejo asked him how he structured his novel: «A partir de una frase que dice: 'Muchos años después, frente al pelotón de fusilamiento, el coronel Aureliano Buendía había de recordar aquella tarde remota en que su padre lo llevó a conocer el hielo.' Tú sabes que eso es tan cierto, te voy a contar. La primera idea que tuve yo de *Cien años de soledad,* la primera imagen—porque yo lo primero que tengo de un libro es una imagen, no es una idea o un concepto, es una imagen—es la de un viejo que lleva a un niño a conocer el hielo.»[1] The structure of *CAS* may very well have started from this image, but it also completes an evolution initiated in *H.* In a conversation with Luis Harss in 1967, García Márquez discussed this point: «*Cien años de soledad* será como la base del rompecabezas cuyas piezas he venido dando en los libros precedentes. Aquí están dadas casi todas las claves. Se conoce el origen y el fin de los personajes, y la historia completa, sin vacíos, de Macondo. Aunque en esta novela las alfombras vuelan, los muertos resucitan y hay lluvias de flores, es tal vez el menos misterioso de todos mis libros, porque el autor trata de llevar al lector de la mano para que no se pierda en ningún momento ni quede ningún punto oscuro. Con éste, termino el ciclo de Macondo, y cambio por completo de tema en el futuro.»[2] The structural components in *CAS,* whether assimilated from earlier works or newly created, are closely linked to the cycle of Macondo which concludes in *CAS.*

Much critical attention has focused on *CAS*'s circular structure, but circularity already appears in *H* and *FMG.* In *H,* both story lines begin at the end. The prologue chronicles Macondo's rise and fall in microhistoric terms, and its last sentence indicates Macondo's moribund state as the novel opens. Macondo is transformed into a static, immobile center around which the doctor's story and Macondo's adumbrated past rotate. Macondo's immobility is both relative and absolute in *H,* and on its circular periphery the two story lines move from their ends back to their beginnings. The doctor and Macondo are both «dead,» and they are brought back to «life» by the circular narrative. At the end, they rejoin their initial states of immobility, for neither story is completed. The circular structure of *H* can be diagrammed as follows:

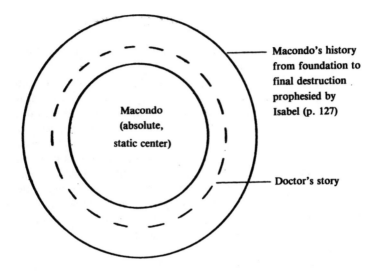

H's circular structure, because of its multiple perspectives, sets in motion several circles. García Márquez has broken down his novel into small units which are reorganized to produce a discontinuous series of juxtaposed frames that reveal the two story lines. He makes no attempt to integrate the two circular story lines whose fragments rotate around the novel's static center in different orbits.

In *FMG,* the circular pattern again revolves around the static center of Macondo, but some important changes have taken place. Like the prologue in *H,* the first two paragraphs summarize the story of Big Mamá's funeral, and the story begins at the end. The difference between *H*'s prologue and the first page of *FMG* is that, in the latter, the story line is the same as Macondo's. It can thus be diagrammed·

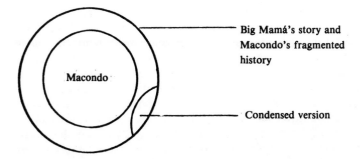

The smaller circle merges with the larger circle which is the sum total of the points (events) located along the circular narrative. The use of a single narrator also explains why only one circle is needed to represent *FMG's* structure. The actual narration of the story rushes along after the first page, and the narrator provides precise temporal indications. The illusion of linearity is undermined by the elimination of dates, and the story is governed more by succession than chronology. The story follows a pattern of death-life-death or end-beginning-end and fulfills the circular imperative of the opening page. Circularity is also evidenced by the presence of fragmentary allusions to Macondo's past and the invitation to retell the same story near the end. In *FMG*, García Márquez integrates the story line of Big Mamá's funeral with Macondo's circularity, and Macondo's space is now «temporalized» because it coincides with the movement of the story. Macondo has thus retained its role as an absolute mythical center but, as a setting for a story, it has achieved mobility.

If *H* is the true antecedent of *CAS*, it is more in terms of the gross constituents than in the actual articulation of the myth of Macondo or in its structure. *FMG* offers more structural and mythical affinities with *CAS*. What is clear is that *CAS* gathers up the strands from his previous works and combines them into a fictional whole. As Vargas Llosa says, «esta novela integra en una síntesis superior a las ficciones anteriores, construye un mundo de una riqueza extraordinaria, agota este mundo y se agota con él.»[3] Another characteristic of *CAS* is «su accesibilidad ilimitada, su facultad de estar al alcance, con premios distintos pero abundantes para cada cual. El genio literario de nuestro tiempo suele ser hermético, minoritario y agobiante. *Cien años de soledad* es uno de los raros casos de obra literaria mayor contemporánea que todos pueden entender y gozar.»[4] The novel's structure contains a built-in principle of expansion which erases the distinction between fiction and myth. The novel transmits its story on the level of Lévi-Strauss' *super-langue;* that is «that however the myth is told, we sense, behind the individual telling or *parole,* and behind the *langue* from which that *parole* derives, a kind of *super-langue,* which emits a fundamental message.»[5] This signifies that «the full reference of myth is always to the conscionable totality of identified experience, and the story told should be understood as making complete sense only when placed in combination with all the other myths.»[6] As Berthoff states, and this applies to *CAS,* «the work of fiction, in brief, has most authority which most abundantly opens itself to the modality of the mythic.»[7]

CAS is an open-structured novel, but it also contains a linear story of the Buendía family and the complete history of Macondo. Both story lines merge, and the reader can discern a beginning, middle and end. The structural problem to be resolved is how circularity and linearity coexist within the same framework. *CAS*'s *parole,* or linearity, is constituted by the story of the Buendía clan and the particular history of Macondo. *Langue* represents the whole culture with its systems and general laws. The myth of Macondo is told first in Sanskrit (compiled by Melquíades) and then in Spanish. Since Sanskrit and Spanish are Indo-European languages and Spanish is the linguistic expression of Hispanic culture, the myth of Macondo reflects both Latin American culture and Western civilization. The *super-langue,* or metalinguistic message, is the myth of Macondo. The structural coexistence of linearity *(parole)* and circularity *(super-langue)* can be explained by applying the principle of *bricolage* and analyzing *CAS*'s external and internal structures.

When Gastón starts to talk with Aureliano, he is amazed at his knowledge, and when «le preguntó cómo había hecho para obtener informaciones que no estaban en la enciclopedia, recibió la misma respuesta que José Arcadio: 'Todo se sabe'» (p. 322). This «everything is known» can be divided into external and internal structures. External structures refer to the overall patterns found by readers and critics, and the first one is the story of the Buendía clan from its foundation to its final destruction. Others include mythical, Biblical, sociological, economic and political models. All these structures concentrate on *what CAS* communicates, but they do not take into account the internal, structural components of *what* is known. An examination of *CAS*'s internal parts, or chapters, provides a more precise idea of its structure. It is composed of twenty unnumbered chapters, and an analysis of the first two demonstrates how circularity, linearity and *bricolage* function throughout *CAS*.

[Chapter 1 constitutes a paradigm, or «protonovela,» of the novel's internal structure. It opens with an allusion to a future and past event: «Muchos años después, frente al pelotón de fusilamiento, el coronel Aureliano Buendía había de recordar aquella tarde remota en que su padre lo llevó a conocer el hielo» (p. 9). The next sentence then plunges back into the remote past: «Macondo era entonces una aldea de veinte casas de barro y cañabraba construidas a la orilla de un río de aguas diáfanas que se precipitaban por un lecho de piedras pulidas, blancas y enormes como huevos prehistóricos» (p. 9). The narrative of the chapter's events starts here: the comings and goings of the gypsies, the idyllic nature of Macondo, the discoveries and experiments of José Arcadio Buendía, his quixotic journey, his alchemical experiments, the infancy of José Arcadio and Aureliano, the aging of Melquíades due to his multiple diseases, the arrival in Macondo of new gypsies and the announcement of Melquíades' death. There is also another reference to Colonel Aureliano Buendía standing before the firing squad (p. 21). The last event in the chapter recounts Aureliano Buendía's discovery of ice. As Vargas Llosa says, the pattern of the chapter can be described as a «muda hacia el futuro, muda hacia el pasado remoto y, de allí, trayectoria lineal hasta llegar al dato que sirvió de apertura: el episodio se muerde la cola, comienza y termina en el mismo sitio, sugiere esa idea de totalidad, de cosa acabada que infunde el círculo.»[8] The first chapter thus forms a kind of unit in itself. The fusion of past, present and future implies that the narrated events are detached from any predetermined chronological scheme. They unfold in a chronological order, but it has nothing to do with dates which have been deleted except for two references to Sir Francis Drake (pp. 16, 24) and one to a Spanish «armadura del siglo XV» (p. 10). The circular sequence of events corresponds to Lévi-Strauss' description of the creative act giving rise to myth. Myth starts from a structure and proceeds to construct a set composed of an object and an event. Here the structure is the chapter that contains a sequence of events in which past, present and future coexist simultaneously. The structure is a circle, a self-enclosed form which does not necessarily depend on the following chapters. As Vargas Llosa says, the chapters resemble «un anillo giratorio que permite al narrador mencionar en cualquier momento cualquiera de las instancias temporales de que consta.»[9]

The circularity of the chapter 1 imitates the work which the *bricoleur* performs. Since his work cannot be defined in terms of a specific project, its final outcome cannot be envisaged. If one put the raw materials of the chapter 1 (the events) at his disposal, he may very well end up at the beginning, thus describing a circle. His narrative is also linear because the events are placed in some order. In other words, telling takes precedence over the chronological arrangement of the events. The narrative, after the first sentences, hurtles forward at amazing speed as the reader moves from one event to another. There is no commentary, summary, or preparation, only the simple succession of events. From «El mundo era tan reciente, que muchas cosas carecían de nombre y para mencionarlas había que señalarlas con el dedo» (p. 9), the reader passes to «Todos los años, por el mes de marzo, una familia de gitanos» (p. 9) to a series of demonstrations, and then to José Arcadio Buendía's absurd application of the magnet to looking for gold. Suddenly the reader encounters: «En marzo volvieron los gitanos» (p. 10). Again, the narrator unleashes a series of disparate actions whose causal link is tenuous at best. The narrative then stops momentarily: «Cuando volvieron los gitanos, Ursula había predispuesto contra ellos a toda la población» (p. 14), and another torrent of narration follows. Finally the gypsies return: «Eran gitanos nuevos. Hombres y mujeres jóvenes que sólo conocían su propia lengua» (p. 21). The succesive visits by the gypsies constitute a series of little concentric circles within the global circularity of the first chapter. They follow the same pattern: «a) llegada de los gitanos, y con ellos de Melquíades; b) reacción y entusiasmo de José Arcadio Buendía; c) oposición de Ursula Iguarán; y d) experiencia y fracaso de José Arcadio Buendía.»[10] These references to the gypsies' arrivals are the only events in the chapter which resemble one another. They seem to mark breathing stops in the otherwise dizzying narrative pace. The narrator indiscriminately blends daily, marvelous, fantastic, real, and magic elements and combines them according to the principle of succession. This also applies to the enumeration of different kinds of objects and people, and these enumerations comprise a series of heterogeneous objects put in relation to one another for no logical reason. The new gypsies bring «sus loros pintados de todos los colores que recitaban romanzos italianos, y la gallina que ponía un centenar de huevos de oro al son de la pandereta, y el mono amaestrado que adivinaba el pensamiento, y la máquina múltiple que servía al mismo tiempo para pegar botones y bajar la fiebre, y el aparato para olvidar los malos recuerdos y el emplasto para perder el tiempo, y un millar de invenciones más, tan ingeniosas e insólitas, que José Arcadio Buendía hubiera querido inventar la máquina de la memoria para poder acordarse de todas» (pp. 21-22). The narrator is in the process of creating a *bricolage* structure, by using whatever elements he has at his disposal but never exceeding the boundaries imposed by the raw materials of his narrative. Not only is the *bricolage* structure evident in *how* the narrator proceeds in chapter 1 but also in *what* he narrates.

José Arcadio Buendía works very much like a *bricoleur*. He uses the magnet to «desentrañar el oro de la tierra» (p. 9). When Melquíades tells him the real use of the magnet, he rejects this idea because he «no creía en aquel tiempo en la honradez de los gitanos» (p 9). He used the magnifying glass as a weapon for solar warfare, and «se expuso él mismo a la concentración de los rayos solares y sufrió quemaduras que se convirtieron en úlceras y tardaron mucho tiempo en sanar» (p. 10). Instead of pursuing his work in developing Macondo, he soon dedicated himself to the pursuit of useless projects, «arrastrado por la fiebre de los imanes, los cálculos astronómicos, los sueños de trasmutación y las ansias de conocer las maravillas del mundo» (p. 16). Everything he does either has no practical goal or is utterly absurd. The *bricoleur* also works in this fashion. Although he undertakes projects, there is no guarantee that he will accomplish it in the end. José Arcadio Buendía's *bricolage* approach is evident in his expedition to find a route to put Macondo in contact with the great inventions. Completely ignorant of the geography of the region, he concluded that «la única posibilidad de contacto con la civilizacíon era la ruta del norte» and he «echó en una mochila sus instrumentos de orientación y sus mapas, y emprendió la termeraria aventura» (p. 17). His quixotic journey leads nowhere, ending «frente a ese mar color de ceniza, espumoso y sucio, que no merecía los riesgos y sacrificios de su aventura» (p. 18). He concludes that «Macondo está rodeado de agua por todas partes» (p. 18). All his actions imitate the *bricolage* process by refusing to follow any predetermined logic. As Patricia Tobin says: «Failing to make the orderly distinctions that history and science demand, the men of the Buendía family naturally fail to insert themselves into the mainstream of Western civilization when it comes rushing into Macondo. They strike out, floundering, and their wild gyrations are an index of their incompatibility with any schemes of progress.»[11] Their actions resemble those of the *bricoleur* in that they convert the «efficiency of productive work into the exuberant non-directiveness of play.»[12] The principle of *bricolage* thus fuses the structure of *how* and *what* is narrated.

In chapter 2, *bricolage* functions in a different way. This time the narrator clarifies an even more distant past: the roots of the Buendía lineage. The reader moves from the discovery of ice at the end of the first chapter to the following statement at the beginning of the second chapter: «Cuando el pirata Francis Drake asaltó a Riohacha, en el siglo XVI, la bisabuela de Ursula Iguarán se asustó tanto con el toque de rebato y el estampido de los cañones, que perdió el control de los nervios y se sentó en un fogón encendido» (p. 24). The reader passes immediately from history to a daily occurrence. If he expects this historical detail to be further explained, he is disappointed. It is simply part of the story and is no more important than any other element. As the story of the family tree unfolds, there is an indiscriminate mixture of elements ranging from the daily to the marvelous. For example: «Una tía de Ursula, casada con un tío de José Arcadio Buendía, tuvo un hijo que pasó toda la vida con unos pantalones englobados y flojos, y que murió desangrado después de haber vivido cuarenta y dos años en el más puro estado de virginidad, porque nació y creció con una cola cartilaginosa en forma de tirabuzón y con una escobilla de pelos en la punta» (p. 25). In kernel form, this sentence presents a microhistory which is never expanded. Chronologically, the second chapter should have come first, but the storyteller, who controls a certain number of elements (the story of Macondo and its inhabitants), and who is not encumbered by chronology, can order his story as he wishes.

Chapter 2, which describes the Buendía lineage, their journey from Riohacha, the founding of Macondo, and early life in Macondo, does not have a circular structure like the first chapter. This structural difference confirms that the *bricolage* composition of the novel will present variations from chapter to chapter. After José Arcadio Buendía kills Prudencio Aguilar, the decision is made to undertake the perilous journey «hacia la tierra que nadie les había prometido» (p. 27). The journey is a *bricolage* activity: «No se trazaron un itinerario definido. Solamente procuraban viajar en sentido contrario al camino de Riohacha para no dejar ningún rastro ni encontrar gente conocida. Fue un viaje absurdo» (p. 27). Finally, encamped by the side of a river, José Arcadio Buendía dreamed «esa noche que en aquel lugar se levantaba una ciudad ruidosa con casas de paredes de espejo. Preguntó qué ciudad era aquella, y le contestaron con un nombre que nunca había oído, que no tenía significado alguno pero que tuvo en el sueño una resonancia sobrenatural: Macondo» (p. 28). Like everything the Buendías do, the founding of Macondo represents a *bricolage* act with no apparent justification other than that the name had a supernatural resonance. The story of the Buendía clan is composed of raw materials that are neither explained nor ordered chronologically, but told in the most entertaining manner possible.

The omniscient narrator, whose perspective encompasses past, present and future, alludes to Colonel Aureliano Buendía: «Años después, durante la segunda guerra civil, el coronel Aureliano Buendía trató de hacer aquella misma ruta para tomarse a Riohacha por sorpresa, y a los seis días de viaje comprendió que era una locura» (p. 28). This *bricolage* reference has nothing to do with the present story, but the storyteller decides to include it at this point without further clarification. The new gypsies who arrive are experts in *bricolage*: «Esta vez, entre muchos otros juegos de artificio, llevaban una estera voladora. Pero no la ofrecieron como un aporte fundamental al desarrollo del transporte, sino como un objeto de recreo» (pp. 33-34). Their arrival is as fortuitous as ever: «Ursula había cumplido apenas su reposo de cuarenta días, cuando volvieron los gitanos» (p. 33). One night José Arcadio, enamored with a gypsy, accompanied them when they left Macondo. No great consternation is caused by his departure, the Buendías proceed in a *bricolage* manner, and time «puso las cosas en su puesto» (p. 37). The structure of the novel incorporates everything and treats it with the same uniform objectivity. As if by chance, «de pronto, casi cinco meses después de su desaparición, volvió Ursula» (p. 38), and the structure reincorporates a previously told incident. José Arcadio Buendía, who had tried in vain to discover the route leading to civilization and great inventions, learns that Ursula, by chance, discovered it. The narrator recombines events in order to produce *bricolage* structuring of all the efforts and actions of the different characters.

The analysis of the first two chapters raises important points. First, each chapter is a self-contained unit. Neither the relationship between the structures of chapters 1 and 2 nor the sequence in which the events unfold has anything to do with a preconceived, chronological plan. The structure of *CAS* builds upon each event until a chapter is formed, and each chapter is a building block unlike the others. Just as the internal structure of each chapter is discontinuous, so too is the succession of chapters. The horizontal story line in *CAS* is the axis along which the narrator builds up his *bricolage* structures which are composed of a «set of tools and materials (the Buendía family history) which is always finite and is also heterogeneous because what it contains bears no relation to the current project, or indeed to any particular project.»[13] Because of the choices made by the narrator, the entire structure of the novel exhibits discontinuity from chapter to chapter. Certain patterns such as circularity repeat themselves, but, basically, no single pattern dominates. The story is still linear, but the particular ordering of events depends on the *bricolage* technique which emphasizes succession, relationships and discontinuity over order, logic and chronology.

Structurally, the first two chapters set in motion several operating principles which characterize *CAS's* overall, internal organization. Chapter 1 introduces the principle of circularity on two levels: 1) the overall structure of the chapter (Colonel Aureliano Buendía's discovery of ice); and 2) the series of smaller, concentric circles constituted by the gypsies' repeated visits. This circularity also coincides with the establishment of Macondo as the absolute, immobile center around which the story of the Buendías and Macondo gravitates. The linearity of the first chapter is represented by the succession of events leading to the discovery of ice. Chapter 1 succeeds in combining linearity *(parole),* circularity *(super-langue),* the Center (Macondo as timeless, stationary center), and Macondo as a setting for a version of the myth of Macondo. García Márquez, however, suspends the linear telling of the version until the second chapter. Chapter 1's structure can be diagrammed as follows:

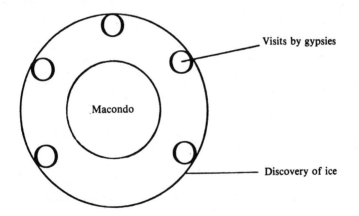

The successive visits by the gypsies also open onto different areas which establish certain constants in *CAS.* The smaller circles not only repeat themselves but bring into play the essential components of the Buendías and Macondo. During the second visit, for example, José Arcadio Buendía's digressive, expansive imagination is revealed, which contrasts with the industrious side of his character. The male descendants will continue this dichotomy. The magic-daily spaces are also implanted in chapter 1. Ursula, who creates the daily space, is constantly opposed to Melquíades whose presence and influence create the magical space. These repeated visits also link the structure of the novel to the vital cycles of life, for each visit, precisely in-dicated, «es el índice de esa continuación de la vida, pero cada vez más rica. Ellos llegan y traen nuevos elementos fabulosos que enriquecen de fantasía ese mundo recién creado.»[14] The first chapter thus organizes time and space in the same way as Lévi-Strauss' triadic structure of myth. Chapter 1 constitutes a *bricolage* process in which heterogeneous elements combine to form its structure. Linearity, cir-cularity, Macondo the mythical place, and also the setting for the story, and the Buendía clan all find their place in a structure dominated by the idea of the relationship that these components have to each other. The structure of chapter 1 is permutable; that is, the constituent elements are «capable of standing in successive relations with other entities—although with only a limited number and only on the condition that they always form a system in which an alteration which affects one element automatically affects all the others.»[15] The *bricolage* structure of chapter 1 is also modifiable because, like myth, which consists of a limited number of elements that are constantly rearranged from version to version, its finite elements can also be reordered by the storyteller. The *bricoleur* also arranges and re-arranges the elements at his disposal so that, if his task were to con-struct chapters, he would produce a series of discontinuous ones dif-fering greatly in structure.

The structure of chapter 2 employs linearity as its basic organi-zing principle, and *parole* really starts here; that is, the variant of the myth of Macondo. The chapter is organized around the two journeys (pp. 27 and 36), and they serve the same function as the gypsies' visits: to introduce new elements into the novel. Also the return of the gyp-sies plays no role in the chapter's structure: «A diferencia de la tribu de Melquíades, habían demostrado en poco tiempo que no eran heraldos del progreso, sino mercachifles de diversiones» (p. 33). The structure of chapter 2 can be diagrammed in the following manner:

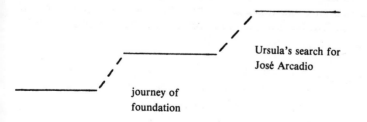

At each point where a journey is undertaken, the linear structure moves to another level since new elements are introduced. After the first journey, Pilar Ternera appears. When Ursula returns, she brings the fruits of civilization which José Arcadio Buendía had been unable to find. The discontinuity of chapters 1 and 2 harmonizes with the *bricolage* structure of the novel, for diverse structural patterns can coexist within its boundaries. The structure of *CAS* is not limited to one principle, and it is composed of circles and lines which produce a discontinuous, permutable pattern which not only varies from chapter to chapter, but within each chapter.

Since one of *CAS*'s central themes is circularity, the circle is also the most appropriate figure to represent the novel's internal structure. It emphasizes *CAS*'s self-sufficiency, for everything is enclosed within its limits. Each chapter represents a spin of the narrative wheel which produces an entity which stands in discontinuous and successive relationship to the other chapters. Vargas Llosa, who distinguishes fourteen loops in time within the narrative structure, compares the novel's structure to an «anillo giratorio» which resembles «un gran círculo compuesto de numerosos círculos, contenidos unos dentro de otros, que se suceden, superponen y encabalgan, y que son de diámetros diferentes.»[16] Patricia Tobin improves on his circle by adding «'a circle with a twist in it.' The figure is a Moebius strip, a band which is given a half-twist before its ends are pasted together to form a circle, so that its 'two sides' are always one surface.»[17] She explains that «along this single surface (the metonymical axis) are played the conversions, permutations, reorientations, and transformations of the pluralistic 'everything,' which genealogical order would have separated into the *either/or* categories of logical thought. The superior significance of the twist lies in its conversions of the inside to the outside, the central to the peripheral, which in their representation of disorder offer for our contemplation other possible orders contrary to the actual.»[18] The Moebius strip analogy provides a clear image of *CAS*'s *bricolage* form which becomes a kinked circle as the discontinuous structure performs its visible twists and turns throughout *CAS*. Since CAS's structure is discontinuous and permutable, these twists and turns clearly resemble the pattern produced by the *bricoleur*.

Bricolage provides the operating principle whereby *CAS* becomes an open-structured novel governed by the law of discontinuity. Because of its principle of generosity, it includes *all* of the elements in its instrumental set, and it emphasizes arrangement, reordering, and the permutable relationships between elements over order, efficiency, and predetermined patterns. The structure it produces, like the different versions of myth, is discontinuous and alterable in relation to any ideal structure the elements might have. Each chapter is an individual entity which stands in discontinuous and successive relationship to every other chapter, and, within each chapter, the same principles function. Circles and lines characterize the asymmetrical configuration of this structure, and they are strung together in a *bricolage* manner. This does not mean that they are either mutually exclusive, or complementary, but that they coexist within a changeable, organic structure which constantly twists and turns in relation to its static reference point which is Macondo. *Bricolage* unites the triadic nature of myth, interweaving *parole, langue,* and *super-langue* to produce an open-structured novel of great accessibility and readability.

NOTES

1. E. González Bermejo, «Ahora 200 años de soledad,» *Oiga,* No. 392 (Septiembre, 1970, Lima), p. 31.

2. Luis Harss, «La cuerda floja,» in: *Sobre García Márquez,* ed. Pedro Simón Martínez (Montevideo: Biblioteca de Marcha, 1971), p. 24.

3. Mario Vargas Llosa, *García Márquez: historia de un deicidio* (Barcelona: Barral Editores, 1971), p. 479.

4. *Ibid.,* p. 480.

5. Terence Hawkes, *Structuralism and Semiotics* (London: Methuen & Co. Ltd., 1977), p. 44.

6. Warner Berthoff, *Fictions and Events: Essays in Criticism and Literary History* (New York: E. P. Dutton & Co., Inc. 1971), p. 49.

7. *Ibid.,* p. 54.

8. Vargas Llosa, p. 550.

9. Vargas Llosa, p. 548.

10. José Miguel Oviedo, Hugo Achugar and Jorge Arbeleche, *Aproximación a Gabriel García Márquez* (Montevideo: Fundación de Cultura Universitaria, 1969), pp. 23-24.

11. Patricia Drechsel Tobin, *Time and the Novel: The Genealogical Imperative* (Princeton: Princeton University Press, 1978), p. 169.

12. *Ibid.,* p. 170.

13. Claude Lévi-Strauss, *The Savage Mind* (Chicago: The University of Chicago Press, 1970), p. 17.

14. José Miguel Oviedo, p. 28.

15. Lévi-Strauss, p. 20.
16. Vargas Llosa, p. 550.
17. Tobin, p. 176.
18. *Ibid.,* p. 176.

THE BANANA MASSACRE: A MICROSTRUCTURAL EXAMPLE OF *BRICOLAGE* AND MYTH

CHAPTER 4

The twenty chapters of *CAS* form its macrostructure, and the events of each chapter represent microstructures. An analysis of the massacre of the banana workers demonstrates the *bricolage* process at the microstructural level. For the banana massacre, García Márquez relied on a specific historical source, and it differs from the other events in the detailed treatment that he devotes to it. The narrative flow is interrupted by the sudden presence of realistic detail so much in contrast to what has preceded. The banana massacre involves three levels of reality delineated by Alan Schweitzer: (1) the historical, immediate level of factual, linear time; (2) psychological, i.e., subjective time; and (3) mythical or ahistorical time. [1] The first level relates «to the arbitrary reproduction, in narrative form, of a hypothetical yet highly credible American landscape and the ensuing ethos of its inhabitants.» [2] The second «recreates and sublimates that ethos as revealed intuitively by the central characters.» [3] The third level «prefigures a transcendental, paradigmatic order which realizes its cyclic continuity through the collective generational sequence of the principal characters.» [4] Each level contributes to understanding how *bricolage* functions at the microstructural level.

It is clear that García Márquez read and incorporated Carlos Cortés Vargas' version of the banana massacre. He was the acting provincial military commander when the event took place on December 6, 1928. García Márquez retains the general sequence described by Cortés Vargas, and a comparison of the two versions reveals their similarities. Cortés Vargas states that «los amotinados al apercibir la presencia de las tropas intensificaron sus gritos.»⁵ After deploying his troops to prevent any surprise attack, Captain Julio Garavito read «el Decreto No. I de la jefatura Civil y Militar» (p. 239). After advising the crowd to return to their homes, «esas palabras fueron contestadas con grandes gritos» (p. 239). The crowd was given five minutes to withdraw, during which time no one moved. Finally, the captain warned them that firing would commence after one more minute. As the last warning sounded, the «multitud parecía clavada en el suelo» (p. 239). When the firing started, «la masa humana cayó como un solo hombre» (p. 239). «La tropa,» Cortés Vargas continues, «con admirable disciplina, no disparó un cartucho más» (p. 239). After the cease-fire order, the crowd «se levantó y huyó dejando el suelo literalmente cubierto de machetes, sombreros y algunas prendas de vestir» (p. 239). Because the soldiers fired above the crowd, «fueron muy pocas las bajas que sufrió el pueblo» (p. 240). Owing to the early hour (1:30 A. M.) there were no women or children present according to Cortés Vargas. He further states that «la gran mole de los amotinados que venía de la Zona, en esos precisos momentos, estaba ya llegando a la población; diez minutos de demora y habría habido centenares de víctimas, muchas de ellas inocentes» (p. 240). As a result, «Nueve (9) hombres quedaron muertos» (p. 240).

In García Márquez' version, due to the gravity of the situation, the authorities «hicieron un llamado a los trabajadores para que se concentraran en Macondo» (p. 257). It was announced that «el Jefe Civil y Militar de la provincia llegaría el viernes siguiente, dispuesto a interceder en el conflicto» (p. 257). José Arcadio Segundo was in the crowd which awaited the arrival of the Civil and Military Commander of the province. He had previously taken part in a «reunión de los dirigentes sindicales y había sido comisionado junto con el coronel Gavilán para confundirse con la multitud y orientarla según las circunstancias» (p. 257). The army had placed «nidos de ametralladoras alrededor de la plazoleta» (p. 258). Then the crowd, composed of «más de tres mil personas, entre trabajadores, mujeres y niños» (p. 258), overflowed into the side streets «que el ejército cerró con filas de ametralladoras» (p. 258). The crowd tolerated the wait for the military commander's arrival in a festive manner until the rumor spread that the train would not arrive until the following day. As the crowd grew more agitated and impatient, a woman asked José Arcadio Segundo to put one of her children on his shoulders so that he could better hear the reading of the «Decreto Número 4 del Jefe Civil y Militar de la provincia» (p. 258) which was signed by General Carlos Cortés Vargas and his secretary, Enrique García Isaza. The child «había de seguir contando, sin que nadie se lo creyera, que había visto al teniente leyendo con una bocina de gramófono» /the Decree/ (p. 258). Even after warnings were issued to the crowd to disperse, it remained motionless. José Arcadio Segundo, convinced that nothing would incite the crowd to act, shouted «Cabrones!. . . falta». Les regalamos el minuto que falta'» (p. 259). The order was given to fire and fourteen machine guns responded in unison, but «todo parecía una farsa» (p. 259). After an initial moment of immobility, «una fuerza sísmica, un aliento volcánico, un rugido de cataclismo, estallaron en el centro de la muchedumbre con una descomunal potencia expansiva» (p. 259). Instead of heeding the warning to lie on the ground, «los sobrevivientes trataron de volver a la plazoleta, y el pánico dio entonces un coletazo de dragón, y los mandó en una oleada compacta contra la otra oleada compacta que se movía en sentido contrario, despedida por el otro coletazo de dragón de la calle opuesta, donde también las ametralladoras disparaban sin tregua» (pp. 259-60). Enclosed in a circle of fire, the people were «sistemáticamente recortados en redondo, como pelando una cebolla, por las tijeras insaciables y metódicas de la metralla» (p. 260). José Arcadio Segundo, wounded, faints and later awakens on a train transporting the dead bodies to the sea where they would be dumped.

García Márquez even includes, either verbatim or in modified form, certain sentences found in the official account: «Tienen cinco minutos para retirarse» (the same in both accounts: Valdeblánquez, p. 239, *CAS*, p. 258); «pasados los cinco minutos se dio un toque corto. 'Un minuto más y se romperá el fuego', gritó el Capitán» (Valdeblánquez, p. 239); «'Han pasado cinco minutos' dijo el capitán en el mismo tono, 'Un minuto más y se hará fuego'» (*CAS*, P. 258). «'Le regalamos el minuto que falta,' gritó una voz de entre el tumulto» (Valdeblánquez, p. 239); «'Cabrones,' gritó José Arcadio Segundo. 'Les regalamos el minuto que falta'» (*CAS*, p. 259); «una voz dentro de la multitud gritó al mismo tiempo 'Tenderse'» (Valdeblánquez, p. 239); «Varias voces gritaron al mismo tiempo: 'Tírense al suelo! Tírense al suelo!'» (*CAS*, p. 259). These summaries reveal the conflict between the official historical version and the fictionalized account. García Márquez did not witness the massacre, and Cortés Vargas is dead, so how can the final, definitive version of the event be established? This is obviously an impossible task because complete, historical objectivity is an illusion. Any past event is subject to a multitude of viewpoints which historians cannot possibly record for the lack of documentation. García Márquez would have only engaged in an exercise in futility if he had tried to dispute the historical accuracy of Cortés Vargas' version, since the latter witnessed and participated in the event.

García Márquez, aware of the fact that Cortés Vargas' historical account represents only one version, sought to create a fictional event which simultaneously retained the basic framework of the historical account and presented another variant. In Cortés Vargas' version, the historical, military and official perspective de-emphasizes its human content. Even the historian, José María Valdeblánquez, presents opposing viewpoints whose validity he disputes: « En el presente libro de historia, tratándose de un episodio trágico como el que se derivó de la huelga de la zona bananera, que aunque acaecida en mi Departamento del Magdalena y, propiamente, en el Municipio de Ciénaga, tuvo repercusiones nacionales, no podía prescindir del estudio exhaustivo de los antecedentes de esa tragedia que observé personalmente, ya que me anima el propósito de hacer conocer de toda Colombia, con la mayor exactitud posible, esa situación sufrida por los magdalenenses. Y me expreso ligeramente así porque la generalidad de las gentes tiene de esa situación, la impresión, la creencia, y hasta la seguridad de que las víctimas se cuentan por centenares, vecinas al millar, cuando la realidad es que no alcanzaron a la mitad del centenar, en toda la extensión del territorio de la nombrada zona bananera» (p. 235). In an effort to establish complete historical accuracy, he quotes the Communist leader, Alberto Castrillón R.: «Dos ametralladoras y la doble hilera de fusiles reformados habían lanzado sus proyectiles sobre una multitud no menor de 4.000 personas. Un minuto de intervalo y otra descarga igual a retroguardia ahogó las voces de SOCORRO que imploraban piedad. Montones de cadáveres rellenaban la ancha plazoleta, ayes lastimeros, imprecaciones de dolor de vidas que se extinguían, niños de corta edad, mujeres en cinta, jóvenes vigorosos, hombres cuyos brazos habían vivido en alto pregonando la canción del trabajo, ancianos que otrora ayudaron con su sangre a la conquista de la libertad, cayeron allí, no ajusticiados por la patria, sino asesinados de manera cobarde por un hombre que hubiera deshonrado a las huestes de Atila» (p. 240). In order to discredit any other possible interpretations, Valdeblánquez presents a mass of documentary evidence with titles such as «Sigue el relato del general Cortés Vargas,» «El gerente en rebeldía con la ley hace concesiones,» «El gerente de la United informa al Ministro de Guerra,» «Sentencia condenatoria contra Alberto Castrillón R.,» etc. All this material is designed to support and justify the historical accuracy of Cortés Vargas' version. Finally, to insure the validity of his account, Valdeblánquez recalls a later encounter with Cortés Vargas so he can solidify the *before* and *after* of this event: «Años después en la casa del doctor José Jesús García, en Bogotá, Cortés Vargas visitó a Monseñor Joaquín García Benítez, Arzobispo de Medellín, y estando presente este cronista, refirió los mismos episodios que aparecen en su libro, especialmente el momento de la madrugada del 6 de diciembre en que se encaminó a la Estación del Ferrocarril, a disolver a los miles de huelguistas que estaban allí, pues la mitad de la tropa era recluta, y como se aseguraba que la tropa estaba de parte de los revoltosos, él vio la necesidad de asumir el mando del ataque, ante la duda de contar con la confianza de los soldados» (p. 274). García Márquez, confronted by this evidence, yet aware of its internal contradictions, structured the event to achieve two objectives: (1) to recreate an event through an objective narrative which retains its historical verisimilitude; and (2) to undermine the event's historical dimension and causal, linear sequence through a *bricolage* process.

Carlos Cortés Vargas resembles Lévi-Strauss' engineer because he communicates his version in the most efficient way. He defines his project (the telling of the massacre), assembles the precise equipment (position of crowd, troop movements, placement of soldiers, number of wounded and dead, etc.), and carries out his project in the most direct manner (construction of the event according to data governed by his military point of view). Cortés Vargas starts from a series of events and creates a chronological structure. In doing so, he necessarily eliminated many details which did not correspond to his particular perspective. The final result is an event resembling a solid block which eliminates the human dimension. García Márquez' narrator presents the same event as a porous surface constantly penetrated by the human dimension. He works like the *bricoleur* who interrogates all the heteroclite objects of which his treasury is composed in order to discover what each of them could signify, and refuses to exclude anything for the sake of efficiency. Since he already knows the whole Buendía family history, he starts from a structure and constructs a set. The banana massacre belongs to the structure of the family history, and he creates another version of it. The banana massacre's «structure» is the sum total of its components which, like the mythemes of myth, are subject to constant rearrangement. The structure of the historical event is fixed in a chronological sequence, and what changes is the interpretation of this structure. The narrator reorders its components without altering its meaning, which remains the same from version to version.

Cortés Vargas' version presents several interesting points. He never speaks in the first person, and the viewpoint alternates between an objective third person (se ordenó alistar todas las tropas, así se hizo, esas palabras fueron contestadas con grandes gritos, etc.) and the first person plural identified with the military (acto seguido, se sentó la diligencia de posesión, la cual tomamos ante los testigos, nos pusimos, habíamos cumplido, etc.). Cortés Vargas tries to remain objective by declaring that a telegram arrived «con el Decreto Legislativo No. I de 5 diciembre (1928) sobre la declaratoria del estado de sitio en la Provincia de Santa Marta y sobre nobramiento del General Carlos Cortés Vargas, como Jefe Civil y Militar en dicha provincia» (p. 238). The event unfolds in a chronological fashion, and temporal indications mark its progression from beginning to end. It commences at «11 y 30 de la noche» (p. 238) on December 5, 1928. The next indication announces the start of the middle portion of the event: «La columna desembocó por la calle más cercana a la Estación del Ferrocaril. Era la una y media de la madrugada del seis de Diciembre» (p. 239). The internal details of this part are communicated in minutes: «Tiene cinco minutos para retirarse,» «Un minuto más y se romperá el fuego» and «'Le regalamos el minuto que falta,' gritó una voz de entre el tumulto» (p. 239). The potential protraction of the event at this point is compressed between two short phrases: «Fuego!! gritamos», «Alto el fuego!! gritamos» (p. 239). Cortés Vargas maintains a strict chronological framework which does not permit any intrusion of the human dimension. The account ends with an official counting of the dead. His version thus fulfills the requirements of a historical account: an objective viewpoint, a chronological presentation of the event's internal details, the use of temporal indications to mark its chronological progression, and the contraction of time and space to insure the event's solidity.

In *CAS,* the same event undergoes a radical change in its arrangement. It is structured so that the human dimension constantly penetrates the historical framework. The first paragraph, which presents the historical event, starts and ends objectively: «La ley marcial facultaba al ejército para asumir funciones de árbitro de la controversia, pero no se hizo ninguna tira de conciliación» (p. 257); «El llamado anunciaba que el Jefe Civil y Militar de la provincia llegaría el viernes siguiente, dispuesto a interceder en el conflicto» (p. 257). The human dimension breaks through the historical surface at the beginning of the next paragraph: «José Arcadio Segundo estaba entre la muchedumbre que se concentró en la estación desde la mañana del viernes» (p. 257). The narrator then interweaves these two dimensions: «José Arcadio Segundo se acaballó al niño en la nuca. Muchos años después, ese niño había de seguir contando, sin que nadie se lo creyera, que había visto al teniente leyendo con una bocina de gramófono el Decreto Número 4 del Jefe Civil y Militar de la provincia. Estaba firmado por el general Carlos Cortes Vargas, y por su secretario, el mayor Enrique García Isaza, y en tres artículos de ochenta palabras declaraba a los huelguistas *cuadrilla de malhechores* y facultaba al ejército para matarlos a bala» (p. 258). A series of shorter paragraphs describes the massacre, which interfuses the historical and human spheres. As for the end of the massacre, there is none. When José Arcadio Segundo finally makes his way back to Macondo, the event's reality is denied by everyone except him. A woman that he meets says «Aquí no ha habido muertos. Desde los tiempos de tu tío, el coronel, no ha pasado nada en Macondo» (p. 261). The massacre in *CAS* has a beginning, an expanded middle and an ending so ambiguous as to render the whole event retrospectively tenuous and insubstantial. From the outset, the event progressively detaches itself from its linear sequence until it dissipates and fades into the shadows.

The purpose of injecting the human element is to demonstrate that «Colombia's past is as much a fiction as *Cien años de soledad,* all the more so of course because it is contained in words that were written, like the textbook that denies that Macondo ever had a banana plantation, and with the deliberate aim to deceive. So the final pages of *Cien años de soledad,* by showing us how Macondo can exist only within the pages of the book that depicts it, also symbolizes the fact that Colombia's past only exists within the books that have been written about it. Like the history of Macondo, the history of Colombia is a verbal fiction.»[6] This subversion of the historical event is accomplished on a psychological level. By replacing Cortés Vargas with José Arcadio Segundo, García Márquez transfers the point of view to one of the central characters. José Arcadio Segundo's viewpoint opens the door to the human dimension which comes into conflict with chronological history. This conflict can be clarified by using two terms from linguistics: diachronic and synchronic. Diachronic linguistics, which studies the historical evolution of language, corresponds to Cortés Vargas' standpoint which stresses chronological progression. His diachronic stance reaffirms the idea of history as a continuous, logical system composed of events having a *before* and *after*. Synchronic linguistics, which studies language at a given moment in time, corresponds to José Arcadio Segundo's viewpoint. His account emphasizes moments (not necessarily related) rather than linear progression. The massacre has a *before* which is the strike by the banana workers and the ensuing circumstances leading up to the crucial confrontation. At the critical moment of the massacre, José

Arcadio Segundo's synchronic viewpoint initiates the subversion of the event's diachronic, historical solidity. García Márquez' aim is to disrupt chronological history, and, as Lévi-Strauss declares, «each episode resolves itself into a multitude of individual psychic movements. Each of these movements is the translation of unconscious development, and these resolve themselves into cerebral, hormonal or nervous phenomena, which themselves have reference to the physical or chemical order. Consequently, historical facts are no more *given* than any others. It is the historian, or the agent of history, who constitutes them by abstraction and as though under the threat of an infinite regress.»[7]

García Márquez indicates these psycho-chemical reactions at different points in José Arcadio Segundo: «No se sentía bien, y amasaba una pasta salitrosa en el paladar, desde que advirtió que el ejército había emplazado nidos de ametralladoras alrededor de la plazoleta» (pp. 257-58); «José Arcadio Segundo, sudando hielo, se bajó al niño de los hombros y se lo entregó a la mujer» (p. 258); «Embriagado por la tensión, por la maravillosa profundidad del silencio y, además, convencido de que nada haría mover a aquella muchedumbre pasmada por la fascinación de la muerte, José Arcadio Segundo se empinó por encima de las cabezas que tenía enfrente, y por primera vez en su vida levantó la voz» (p. 259). The psycho-chemical reaction, «sudando hielo,» establishes José Arcadio Segundo's indissoluble conscious and unconscious link with the Buendía lineage. The first sentence of the novel reveals the importance of ice as an element linking all the Buendías. Ice serves as a mediator between objective and subjective, diachronic and synchronic, and finally, between chronological and human history. As J. E. Cirlot states: «Given that water is the symbol of communication between the formal and informal, the element of transition between different cycles, it follows that ice represents principally two things: first, the change induced in water by the cold—that is, the 'congelation' of its symbolic significance; and secondly, the stultification of the potentialities of water. Hence ice has been defined as the rigid dividing-line between consciousness and unconsciousness.»[8] Ice, then, acts as a dividing line between the diachronic and synchronic views of the event, which José Arcadio Segundo, by sweating ice, then fuses. García Márquez also suggests the human dimension on a collective level by amplifying Carlos Cortés Vargas' sentence describing the crowd's reaction at the moment of firing («La masa humana cayó como un solo hombre»), and devaluating the historical event.

García Márquez assails the historical event, not in its beginning, but in its end. The process by which he disrupts the historical event resembles a gigantic circular movement which starts, stops and restarts continuously until it finally grinds to a halt at the end of the novel. Each event is a product of the narrative «rueda giratoria,» and blends with the following one, but there is no demonstrable, causal connection between them. He first constructed a historical framework including specific realistic details. He then inserted physico-psychological elements on an individual and collective level which created the human dimension. By linking José Arcadio Segundo's individual reactions to the Buendía family, García Márquez overcomes the problem of including a multitude of human reactions. From the moment José Arcadio Segundo awakens, the reader is plunged into a sort of ahistorical antechamber whose reality remains forever in doubt. All details concerning how long he slept, what happened after he fainted, how he got on the train, etc., are omitted, and the nocturnal ambience reinforces the ambiguity. When he finally makes his way back to Macondo, another reality confronts him: the complete disappearance of any trace of the original historical event. Not even his twin brother, Aureliano Segundo, «creyó la versión de la masacre ni la pesadilla del tren cargado de muertos que viajaba hacia el mar» (p. 262). When the soldiers come looking for the remnants of the rebels, José Arcadio Segundo hides in Melquíades' room piled high with parchments. When the soldiers enter the room, «había la misma pureza en el aire, la misma diafanidad, el mismo privilegio contra el polvo y la destrucción que conoció Aureliano Segundo en la infancia, y que el coronel Aureliano Buendía no pudo percibir» (p. 264). José Arcadio Segundo recognizes in the officer who looks without seeing him a strange affinity with Colonel Aureliano Buendía: «Cuando les habló a los soldados, entendió Aureliano Segundo que el joven militar había visto el cuarto con los mismos ojos con que lo vio el coronel Aureliano Buendía» (p. 265). This revelation leads him to conclude that «el coronel Aureliano Buendía no fue más que un farsante o un imbécil. No entendía que hubiera necesitado tantas palabras para explicar lo que se sentía en la guerra, si con una sola bastaba: miedo» (p. 265). Melquíades' room serves as a converging point for the ancestral skeins joining all the Buendías. By a kind of ancestral transmigration, the banana massacre was a direct result of the civil war, and José Arcadio Segundo's involvement represented an instinctive response to traits transmitted to him by the Colonel. Aureliano Segundo realized this upon seeing his brother: «Estaba iluminado por un resplandor seráfico. Apenas levantó la vista cuando sintió abrirse la puerta, pero a su hermano le bastó aquella mirada para ver repetido en ella el destino irreparable del bisabuelo. 'Eran más de tres mil'—fue todo cuanto dijo José Arcadio Segundo. 'Ahora estoy seguro que eran todos los que estaban en la estación'» (p. 266). This final statement adds an ironic note of unreality, for it comes from José Arcadio Segundo whose own personal reality is tenuous at best. The historical reality of the massacre is completely detached from the words used to describe it. Rather than ending in any conventional sense, it sinks into the depths of unreality. The pervasive dream-like, supernatural atmosphere of this segment of the event also suggests another level of experience which opens onto the mythical, archetypal dimension.

The passage to this level involves a *bricolage* process which results in a completely different arrangement of the available elements. The reference to José Arcadio Segundo sweating ice links the event to the whole family history and initiates the transfer of the event to a trans-historical, mythical plane. José Arcadio Segundo serves as the bridge between chronological history and myth. Alan Schweitzer explains this process in the following way: «Each character creates his own myth within a specific episode, yet each episode relates to and participates in a greater comprehensive order which determines the continuous ebb and flow of those related lives and activities within a conjectural colony located amidst one of many isolated regions of the South American jungles. The exact location of Macondo, to be sure, is imprecise since the town, like its inhabitants, ultimately tend to be generic and prototypical, whose successive lineage constitutes a world in continuous renovation which adumbrates the cyclic persistence of the universe and which prefigures the myth of the eternal return.»[9] Even though there is a cleavage in the text, José Arcadio Segundo retains his historical specificity. From the moment he sweats ice to the time he awakens on the train, historical specificity still predominates. Only after he awakens does the historical event undergo its complete transformation.

The event's tripartite structure can be summarized in the following manner:

(1) Page 257-58: The presentation of historical data taken directly from Carlos Cortés Vargas' account, creation of a historical framework and information transmitted to the reader by the omniscient narrator.

(2) Page 258-60: Inclusion of historical data from Cortés Vargas, but the event is now depicted from José Arcadio Segundo's point of view. The introduction of the human, psychological dimension and the simultaneous start of the disintegration and *bricolage* reconstruction of the event.

(3) Page 260-66: Total restructuring of the historical event and completion of *bricolage* process. The transfer of the historical event to a transhistorical, mythical plane.

The first two segments pave the way for the third stage in which the transhistorical, mythical and timeless realm can be introduced. The third part denies historical time by negating the event's end, and a kind of timelessness supplants it, stretching the event into infinity, as it were, until it blends with the other events. In other words, the massacre's overall configuration resembles myth by its simultaneous specificity and timelessness. Cortés Vargas' version is enclosed in a system of dates which simultaneously insures its specificity and denies its transcendence. García Márquez' variant escapes this duality by eliminating dates and the end of the event. José Arcadio Segundo's solitary affirmation at the end of the chapter re-emphasizes the timeless realm into which the massacre has entered.

Melquíades' room also helps to create the mythical dimension by serving as a converging point for the whole Buendía clan. As Alan Schweitzer states: «Melquíades' room remains beyond any reference to factual time, suspended in total isolation from the encroaching jungle which threatens to absorb and obliterate the colony. As the novel progresses each successive generation becomes more cognizant of the origin and destiny of the line as it manages to decipher the Sanskrit.»[10] García Márquez uses the symbolic value of the room in an original way. Usually, as Cirlot states, the room is a «symbol of individuality—of private thoughts.»[11] Melquaídes' room provides private refuge for the different Buendías, and José Arcadio Segundo is no exception: «Acostumbrado al ruido de la lluvia, que a los dos meses se convirtió en una forma nueva del silencio, lo único que perturbaba su soledad eran las entradas y salidas de Santa Sofía de la Piedad» (p. 265). The room is described in a way which accentuates its timelessness. Protected «por la luz sobrenatural» (p. 265), it is a room where «nunca llegó el viento árido, ni el polvo ni el calor» (p. 296). Each successive generation of Buendías finds refuge in Melquíades' room precisely because the total history of the clan is contained in the parchments. They resemble Jung's concept of the collective unconscious in which certain myths (i.e., the hero myth), archetypes and images manifest themselves in widely divergent cultures because «all human beings possess similar inborn tendencies to form certain general symbols, and that these symbols manifest themselves through the unconscious mind in myth, dreams, delusions and folklore.»[12]

Whatever the merits or shortcomings of Jung's theory, one aspect is particularly relevant. He states that the «archetype is a tendency to form such representations of a motif-representations that can vary a great deal in detail without losing their basic pattern. They are, indeed, an instinctive *trend,* as marked as the impulse of birds to build nests or ants to form organized colonies.»[13] José Arcadio Segundo repeats inherited patterns transmitted to him by earlier members of the clan. He sweats ice, participates in the banana massacre which «was indirectly motivated by an instinctual response to the will of the demised Col. Aureliano Buendía. José Arcadio Segundo was thus perpetuating an enigmatic ancestral obligation whose origin and significance are contained in the parchments.»[14] Melquíades' room represents the collective unconscious of the Buendía clan and the parchments the sum total of their collective responses. The Buendía males repeat the instinctual patterns of earlier members which have been transmitted to them. Another aspect of Jung's ideas also applies to Melquíades room. When Jung spoke of symbols, he considered them as «static subjects that bear some indirect reference outside themselves,» and the symbol then becomes a «static symbol with dynamic potentialities.»[15] Melquíades' room is a static symbol of the Buendía's collective unconscious, and it only succumbs to the ravages of time when the last member of the clan dies. It functions as a point of contact between historical and human time. As the different Buendías participate in each event, Melquíades' room becomes a focal point which helps disrupt the chronological framework of history. Each event, including the banana massacre, is absorbed and integrated into the ebb and flow of the Buendía's collective unconscious. Consequently, events never end in the conventional sense, but dissipate and disappear into the eddies of the unconscious.

The banana massacre in *CAS* has undergone a series of permutations beginning with the dissolution (not destruction) of the historical account by Cortés Vargas and ending with a transhistorical, mythical version of the same event. Instead of trying to produce just another historical version, García Márquez introduces José Arcadio Segundo, whose individual perspective acts as the agent of subversion of chronological history. García Márquez does resemble the historian in that he selects a specific point of view, but the difference between them resides more in their respective methodologies than in their choice of a point of view. The historian's method is chronological whereas García Márquez' uses *bricolage.* For example, if an event consists of A, B, C, D, E, the historian orders them according to the idea of *before* and *after,* deleting those elements which might disrupt the efficient arrangement of the event. In other words, A will always precede B, B always C, etc., and he includes only those elements necessary to complete his task. The *bricoleur* does not eliminate any element for the sake of efficiency, and his final arrangement is not predetermined. His might be D, A, B, C, E, or E, A, C, D, B, etc., since he works with all the elements he has at his disposal. In terms of the banana massacre, the *bricolage* construction produces a non-event with a beginning and no discernible end. The event, funneled through José Arcadio Segundo's subjectivity, produces a *bricolage* version full of contradictions. José Arcadio Segundo is deeply rooted in the unfolding event, but historical veracity, recorded in words, is quickly supplanted by a subjective perception linked to the collective unconscious of the Buendía clan. What results is the creation of another dimension of time which is both «*parallel* and *homogeneous* to that order of conscious 'factual' time. In this sequence (the banana massacre), as indeed in the novel as a whole, the events emerge in a continuous linear fashion whose uniform flow of succession parallels the factual world of historical reality.»[16] These subjective incursions produce temporal schemes that «are often involuted and sinuous, with frequent distortions of the respective unities of the present, past and future with the result that the time references become ambiguous and indistinguishable. The unfolding narrative on the empirical level is characterized by a continuous process of metamorphoses, a condition which results from the constant infiltration and incursion into that factual order by a distinct category of being. This comprehensive order which infiltrates into the factual, historical world is identified with the expansive consciousness of the protagonists, who, in their intricate interactions occasion a myriad of distinctive perspectives related to each individual character. Yet this vast mosaic of interrelated correspondences constitutes yet a tertiary order of a common *Weltanschauung* in which the inclusive members of the dynasty comprehend a view of totality as projected against the cosmogonic myth.»[17] Thus, each character is both individual and archetypal, each event is both historical and transhistorical. The double structure of each character and event facilitates its transformation into an exemplary character participating in a prototypical event within the context of the myth of Macondo.

NOTES

1. S. Alan Schweitzer, *The Three Levels of Reality in García Márquez' Cien años de soledad* (New York: Ediciones Plaza Mayor, 1972), p. 5.
This chapter was earlier published as: «The Banana Massacre in *Cien años de soledad:* A Micro-structural Example of Myth, History and *Bricolage, Chasqui,* Vol. VIII, No. 3 (Mayo, 1979), pp. 3-23.

2. *Ibid.,* p. 5.

3. *Ibid.,* p. 5.

4. *Ibid.,* p. 5.

5. José María Valdeblánquez, *Historia del departamento del Magdalena y del territorio de la Guajira* (Bogotá Editorial «El Voto Nacional,» 1964), p. 239. All other quotes will come from this edition and page numbers will be given in parentheses.

6. D. P. Gallagher, *Modern Latin American Literature* (New York: Oxford University Press, 1973), pp. 156-57.

7. Claude Lévi-Strauss, *The Savage Mind* (Chicago: The University of Chicago Press, 1970), p. 257.

8. J. E. Cirlot, *A Dictionary of Symbols,* trans Jack Sage (New York: Philosophical Library, Inc., 1962), p. 148.

9. Schweitzer, p. 11.

10. Schweitzer, p. 13.

11. Cirlot, p. 262.

12. C. S. Kirk, *Myth: Its Meaning and Functions in Ancient and Other Cultures* (Berkeley: University of California Press, 1973), p. 275.

13. Carl G. Jung, *Man and his Symbols* (New York: Dell Publishing Co., Inc., 1974), p. 58.

14. Schweitzer, p. 7.

15. Kirk, pp. 278-9.

16. Schweitzer, p. 8.

17. *Ibid.,* pp. 8-9.

THE NARRATOR OF MYTH AND MYTHICAL NARRATION IN *CIEN AÑOS DE SOLEDAD*

CHAPTER 5

As García Márquez' fiction evolves towards *CAS,* his narrators undergo several distinct permutations. In *H,* he experiments with multiple narrators. The doctor's story unfolds from three viewpoints corresponding to three different time perspectives. Although García Márquez does not clearly distinguish between narrators, the reader can identify them and reconstruct the basic outline of the doctor's story. The collection of short stories in *Los funerales de la Mamá Grande* returns to the omniscient, third person narrator except for *FMG* in which the narrator is no longer so cohesive, and the link between the narrator and author is more tenuous. In *FMG,* the third person narrator undergoes a permutation which brings him much closer to the anonymous storyteller of myth. In *CAS,* the narrator changes once again, and the omniscient narrator's prerogatives are restored.

If, as in *FMG,* García Márquez progresses toward a «telling» of a story in *CAS,* then some remarks about the relationship between oral and written literature are needed. Although the author and narrator may indeed be quite different, there is an implicit assumption that «literature was in the first place created by one person speaking to others and that this primal situation of oral performance is still being re-created or imitated by most literary works.»[1] The relationship between oral and written literature is ancient and complex, but the printed word has so much authority in our culture that oral literature has almost disappeared. This oral tradition cannot simply be dismissed as a form associated with primitive, unintelligible utterances.

As Scholes and Kellogg state in *The Nature of Narrative:* «Oral and written narrative are formally distinct, and profoundly so, but they are not culturally distinct in any meaningful way. The sanctity of the printed word in our culture has at times allowed the worst of Socrates' fears to be realized. Words in their printed form have become more real for us than either the sounds on the lips of living men or the concepts they represent. Books as mere physical objects sometimes surpass wisdom in the world's esteem. Any lie or outrage which takes on the dignity of print becomes a thousandfold more menacing. And forgetfulness within themselves has robbed literate men of the ability even to conceive of the production of great literature by unlettered poets and story-tellers.»[2] If *CAS* attempts to close the gap between oral and written literature, then oral literature must be taken into consideration. Oral literature is characterized by «formulaic language, stock scenes, repetitions of themes and motifs, set runs and refrains, standard topoi and metaphors; but surpassing all of these formal characteristics in significance is the fact that the 'work' exists only as it is embodied in performance, is created anew each time it is heard, and therefore has no 'author'.»[3] Oral literature does not depend «on fixed texts that performers memorize. Instead, each performance is a re-creation of a singer's vast store of verbal and literary formulas of a literary work that he and his audience know in an ideal form but have never heard in its entirety and completeness or ever, even incompletely, in the same words twice.»[4] Oral literature is, «like natural language, heavily influenced by convention. An individual oral artist would not attempt to alter traditional verse forms of literary genres in his performance for the same reason a speaker does not consciously attempt to change the grammatical rules of his language. To do so would result in unintelligibility and the consequent hostility of his listeners, with nothing to be gained by the neologism.»[5]

Generally, critics gloss over the question of the narrator in myth since he is assumed to be anonymous. He is reduced to a voice that transmits the content of a given myth, but since our knowledge of most myths exists in written form, the author is impossible to determine. Myth then is treated as part of the prose domain, and little effort is made to analyze and incorporate the importance of orality into the examination of myth. This results in the superimposition of an analytic viewpoint more appropriate to written literature. Dennis Tedlock states that «we shall never develop an effective oral poetics if we begin with the structural analysis of conventional written texts, whether those texts were created by ancient scribes or modern field-workers. Structuralists, attempting to push beyond traditional linguistic frontiers, have 'discovered' eidons, motifemes, mythemes. It is the habit of such reductionist thinking to imagine itself reconstructing, in *reverse,* the actual process by which syllables, words, sentences, and stories were assembled in the factory of the mind. The texts subjected to Lévi-Straussian exposition resembled the pelts and skeletons in zoological archives more than they resembled live animals, right from the moment the analyst laid eyes on them.»[6] Although Tedlock dismisses too quickly the structuralists' contributions, he is right in asserting that the orality of myth has been pushed into the background. Is it possible, however, to approach a literary text as a mediation between the orality of myth and its written form, to examine the work in both its oral and written, mythical dimensions?

Despite the lack of information, a general description of the storyteller can be given. Italo Calvino describes the setting in the following manner: «The tribal storyteller combines sentences and images: the youngest son gets lost in the woods, spots a light in the distance; walks, walks, walks. The tale unfolds sentence by sentence, but where is it heading? Toward the point where something still unspoken, something still only dimly anticipated is revealed, takes hold of us, and tears at us like some man-eating witch. That is when the vibrations of myth pass like a rustling wind through the forest of fairy tales. Myth is the hidden part of every story, the underground part, the zone still unexplored because there are still no words to take us there. The telling of a myth required more than the storyteller's voice at daily tribal gatherings. It required special locations and times, special assemblies. The spoken words were not enough either; there had to be a combination of many-valued signs, i.e. a rite. Myth feeds on silence as much as on the spoken word; a myth makes its presence felt in an ordinary story, in commonplace words; it is like a linguistic void which sucks words into its whirlpool and gives shape to the fable.»[7] Harald Weinrich presents an interesting image of the oral narrator before his audience: «The sophist Protagoras who claims to know how to teach virtue, as well as describe a subject of some importance, is surrounded by listeners; he is probably standing up, or, at the very least, seated in a chair raised above them; the listeners are seated. Socrates is seated with those who have come to learn. Protagoras, proposing his teaching in the form of a myth, adds that he is acting in the same way as the ancients who have the habit of telling tales to the young. He himself is old. We glimpse in this scene a certain function of the mythic narration: although it would not be archetypal, it will serve as a focal point to describe the narrative situation. A situation which envelops the narrator, and around him, a circle of listeners. The narrator is older than his young listeners; he communicates, by his story dealing with a subject of high importance, a wisdom worthy of his age to the young who need this instruction, and this instruction is not unpleasant.»[8] The role of the storyteller described in these two situations depends, in part, on the definition of myth. As Weinrich points out, «this term myth *(mythos)*, as we know, was first a commonly used term for the Greeks which designated any narration, a story told in the market place as well as a story concerning the genealogy of the gods. The term, in its modern usage, can still signify a story of the latter genre, but it no longer serves to designate the insignificant tales of daily life.»[9] The Greek distinction has been maintained in an altered fashion in modern times. Instead of an insignificant story, the popular usage of the word «myth» designates a «false story.» In critical circles the sacred, important function of myth has been retained. Mircea Eliade defines myth as «a sacred history; it relates an event that took place in primordial Time, the fabled time of the 'beginnings.' In other words, myth tells how, through the deeds of Supernatural Beings, a reality came into existence. Myth tells only of that which *really* happened, which manifested itself completely. In short, myths describe the various and sometimes dramatic breakthroughs of the sacred (or the 'supernatural') into the world. It is this sudden breakthrough of the sacred that really *establishes* the World and makes it what it is today.»[10] Northrup Frye, from a literary perspective, defines myth as «a narrative in which some characters are superhuman beings who do things that 'happen only in stories.'»[11] In *Fables of Identity,* however, he states that «myths, as compared with folk tales, are usually in a special category of seriousness: they are believed to have 'really happened,' or to have some exceptional significance in explaining certain features of life, such as ritual.»[12] Lévi-Strauss ascribes to myth the task of mediating a contradiction; that is, it resolves an otherwise logically insoluble situation. The fact that myth critics accord a category of «seriousness» to myth alters the role of the storyteller. His function and presence in relation to his listeners are elevated in comparison to that of a storyteller of a legend or fairy tale. Although it is impossible to recapture the exact narrative situation (gestures, facial expressions, bodily movements, physical posture, etc.), it can be assumed that he is the holder of some fundamental truth which his listeners wish to know.

Whether the storyteller of myth is a member of a primitive tribe or some idealized figure dressed in clothing befitting his station, two important points emerge: the telling (or performance) of the myth and the idea of omniscience. As for performance, Robert Kellogg states: «As a constant behind each performance (in oral literature) is not the mind of an author but an ideal performance, an aspect of the tradition that is shared by performer and audience alike. For this reason the performer in an oral tradition is analogous not to an author but to a skillful reader of written literature. As a written work remains in a kind of limbo until a reader picks it up and 'performs' it, so an oral work exists as an abstract body of rules and ideas until a performer embodies some of them in a performance.»[13] The anonymous, ideal figure of the oral performer interpreting a particular myth finds its equivalent in the modern day reader who «performs» the written text when he reads it. The written text itself is similar to the unperformed oral text, and the idea of the «author» constitutes the whole oral tradition. The supposedly sharp distinctions between oral and written literature may therefore not be as clear as one might imagine. From *H* to *CAS,* the narrator becomes progressively more anonymous, and more closely resembles the storyteller of myth. In modern literature there has been an explosion of voices which narrate the story, but in spite of their invisibility, the reader still assumes the presence of an author. Perhaps the transition from oral to written literature is best seen as a transformation, rather than an elimination, of orality as a form of literature.

The narrative voice in myth finds a close parallel in written literature in the third person, omniscient narrator. The written text makes it difficult not to assume the presence of an author behind each reading. This author's presence disappears in myth because, as Lévi-Strauss has demonstrated, neither the original version of the myth nor its author can be known. Myth is known through its successive versions, but the tellers of these versions, besides their anonymity, also shared the characteristic of omniscience. Their function was to transmit their version, and they were limited by certain linguistic conventions and by the fact that they were working with a limited set of materials. Their freedom derived from the way in which they arranged their materials. Omniscience differs for the storyteller of myth and the third person narrator in written literature. As Kellogg and Scholes explain: «In the case of omniscient narration in the novel, the analogy obscures an important duality in the fictional device. Omniscience includes the related god-like attribute of omnipresence. God *knows* everything because He *is* everywhere—simultaneously. But a narrator in fiction is imbedded in a time-bound artifact. He does not 'know' simultaneously but consecutively. He is not everywhere at once but now here, now there, now looking into this mind or that, now moving on to other vantage points. He is time-bound and space-bound as God is not. Whereas, we conceive of God's omniscience and his omnipresence as being functions of an indivisible quality of godliness, we can separate the omniscient narrator in fiction into a multifarious element and a monistic element. The multiple perceptions of this kind of narrator coalesce into a single reality, a single truth.»[14] The omniscient narrator of fiction does not thus possess the total omniscience of the storyteller, for the latter is not enclosed within any definable temporal boundaries.

In fiction, the storyteller resembles the *histor* who is «the narrator as inquirer, constructing a narrative on the basis of such evidence as he has been able to accumulate. The *histor* is not a character in narrative, but he is not exactly the author himself either. He is a persona, a projection of the author's empirical virtues. Since Herodotus and Thucydides the *histor* has been concerned to establish himself with the reader as a repository of fact, a tireless investigator and sorter, a sober and impartial judge—a man, in short, of authority, who is entitled not only to present the facts as he has established them but to comment on them, to draw parallels, to moralize, to generalize, to tell the reader what to think and even to suggest what he should do.»[15] The storyteller of myth and the *histor* stand in the same relationship to their material, but their respective attitudes towards it differ. The *histor* not only organizes his material according to his own sense of order, but he injects a whole range of interpretations to guide the reader. The storyteller restricts himself to arrangement because myth, as Lévi-Strauss states, communicates its own message which already contains moral and ethical interpretations.

The *histor* and storyteller are similar to Lévi-Strauss' engineer and *bricoleur*. The *histor*-engineer and the *bricoleur*-storyteller both perform a number of tasks, and they are limited by their material. The *histor*-engineer, for the completion of his tasks, subordinates «each of them to the availability of raw materials and tools conceived and procured for the purpose of the project.»[16] If the *histor*'s universe of instruments is a body of facts, he will select or eliminate them in terms of the present project. The *bricoleur*-storyteller, who also works with a finite set of elements (the events of the myth), will not eliminate elements for the sake of efficiency. His universe «of instruments is closed and the rules of his game are always to make do with 'whatever is at hand,' that is to say with a set of tools and materials which is always finite and is also heterogeneous because what it contains bears no relation to the current project, or indeed, to any particular project.»[17] The storyteller-*bricoleur* uses elements which are «'preconstrained' like the constitutive units of myth, the possible combinations of which are restricted by the fact that they are drawn from the language where they already possess a sense which sets a limit on their freedom of manoeuvre.»[18] The storyteller works with events already contained in the previous versions of the myth, but his freedom lies in his telling of the myth. This signifies that he can, within these prescribed limits, reorder the events as long as the basic message of the myth remains intact. The *histor*-engineer arranges his material for purposes which extend beyond the scope of his project since he also interposes himself between his material and his audience and interprets it. The storyteller's method corresponds to Boas' statement that «it would seem that mythical worlds have been built up, only to be shattered again, and that new worlds were built from the fragments.»[19] The storyteller constructs a version of a myth so that «a result can be defined which will always be a compromise between the structure of the instrumental set and that of the project.»[20] When the storyteller's version finally materializes, it inevitably differs from any previous one. In a sense, the storyteller-*bricoleur* never «finishes» his project because the myth will be retold by another storyteller. He thus participates in an ongoing process in which each version represents part of the continuous telling of the myth, but whose message remains the same. The storyteller remains anonymous because he is communicating a preconstrained set of elements, but he may order them in a *bricolage* manner. He does not simply retell the version of an earlier storyteller because, like the *bricoleur,* he «may not ever complete his purpose but he always puts something of himself into it.»[21] These considerations apply directly to the role of the narrator in *CAS.*

The narrator of *CAS* is assigned a rather difficult task: he must retell the whole myth of Macondo. Given the enormity of the task, he must possess the total knowledge of Macondo's history. In *CAS,* the narrator escapes the bonds of time which would limit him to knowing consecutively instead of simultaneously. In the opening sentence, he establishes his global knowledge. The narrator opens with two events which he later completes, then he returns to the remote past. The reader, accustomed to chronology, is disconcerted by this constantly shifting order of events. The narrator, who knows past, present and future, moves along the narrative line frequently jumping back and forth in time without warning. His knowledge extends from the mundane to the miraculous, all of which he narrates with equal neutrality. His neutrality and complete knowledge lead the reader to assume that, like the *histor,* he will provide explanations, commentaries, judgments, feelings, but from beginning to end, the narrator maintains his non-judgmental stance. The reader might also think that he is one of the characters whose age justifies his position. He recalls the third person-first person narrator of Albert Camus's *The Plague* in which the reader discovers at the outset that he is dealing with an internal/external narrator whose identity is later revealed. The narrator, because of his particular posture, is able to present his chronicle of the plague on both an individual and more universal level. No such distinction is drawn in *CAS*.

The narrator's even attitude towards every detail, character, and event remains uniform except for one moment when Fernanda, completely exasperated, bursts into a fiery, accusatory tirade (pp. 274-76). This tirade could indicate the presence of an internal narrator whose identity has yet to be revealed. The problem of the external/internal narrator remains unsolved, but how can such intimate knowledge of characters' thoughts, actions and desires be conveyed in such a detached way? The narrator does not fit the standard definitions of external/internal associated with the relationship between the author and his characters: «The *internal* view opens to us characters' states of mind, reactions and motives, either by narrative report (and judgment, inescapably), by the telling of what in real life would be hidden from an observer, or by one of the more dramatized soliloquy-like 'stream of consciousness' or 'interior monologue' techniques. The *external* perspective accepts the privacy of other people's experience: the writer constructs, for himself and thus for us, the role of an unprivileged observer coming to partial understanding of the fictional figures in a fragmentary way.»[22] In a sense, the narator in *CAS* combines the internal/external perspectives and then modifies them. He narrates the thoughts, desires and actions of the characters like an internal narrator, but he does it from an external perspective. Not only does he respect the privacy of other people's experiences, but he never makes any judgments, commentaries or offers any evidence that he even can know.

The reader might also identify the narrator with Melquíades and then with García Márquez. According to this narrative scheme, the narrator would be a persona of the author, and Melquíades would narrate from within the framework of the novel. This would explain the internal/external division, but, upon closer scrutiny, this assumption proves very problematic. The only certainty is that, as Roger Fowler points out, «inescapably, a narrative text implies through its wording a narrating voice, the tone of an implicit speaker taking a line on his subject and adopting a stance towards his readers.»[23] Whatever the degree of closeness or distance between the author and the narrator, there exists an implicit assumption on the part of the reader that the narrator is the creation of the author. In *CAS,* for example, the reader, aware that García Márquez is a socialist and anti-military, might think that he is conveying this message through his description of the soldiers present during the banana massacre: «Todos eran idénticos, hijos de la misma madre, y todos soportaban con igual estolidez los fusiles con las bayonetas caladas, y el incordio de la obediencia ciega y el sentido del honor» (p. 257). Simple narration thus tends to reveal a certain attitude, but it does not solve the problem of who is narrating in *CAS.*

At the end of *CAS,* the reader learns that Melquíades had written the story of the Buendía clan «hasta en sus detalles más triviales, con cien años de anticipación. La había redactado en sánscrito, que era su lengua materna, y había cifrado los versos pares con la clave privada del emperador Augusto, y los impares con claves militares lacedemonias» (p. 349). He also «no había ordenado los hechos en el tiempo convencional de los hombres, sino que concentró un siglo de episodios cotidianos, de modo que todos coexistieran en un instante» (p. 350). Since Melquíades did not write the same story in Spanish, the narrator performed this function. Their apparently parallel acts differ in one important way: Melquíades' parchments remain undeciphered until the final pages, but the narrator's version of the Buendía family is both a writing and a telling. The parchments serve both an internal and an external function, for they belong to *CAS*'s narrative and represent part of the story. As such, they have no extension beyond themselves. In an external sense, they represent the quest of the narrator which is quite simply to «contarlo todo.» They hold the key to this world which García Márquez has been trying to narrate since he started to write. If *CAS* unites all the skeins of his earlier fiction, then the novel itself is one huge parchment to be deciphered through telling. The parchments also increase the reader's interest in the possible identity of the narrator.

The final pages of the novel leave the matter unresolved, for the narrator and the narrative disappear. All that is revealed is that in the parchments «se contenía la novela, que son la novela; por eso el arduo empeño de leerlos no puede lograrse hasta que las profecías fueron cumplidas, y el narrador, por sus pasos contados, describió ese cumplimiento. El se limita a contar; ni predice el futuro ni posee la clave del pasado.»[24] The reader cannot be certain that Melquíades is the narrator, for he vanishes like everything and everyone else at the end. It is possible that Melquíades is a reflexion, or reincarnation, of the omniscient narrator, for both perform similar tasks. As Gullón points out, no discrepancy exists between the two chronicles: «La una es reproducción literal de la otra, por milagro semejante al acontecido cuando Pierre Menard reescribe, sin saberlo, un *Quijote* idéntico al de Cervantes.»[25] Melquíades resembles the anonymous narrator as a «figura legendaria y mítica, /quien/ posee especiales poderes y en la novela desempeña múltiples funciones.»[26] Gullón points out other ways in which the two resemble each other: «Al principio no sabemos en qué consiste esa diferencia, aun cuando notamos su desarraigo, su vivir en disponibilidad para la ausencia, y tenemos la sensación de que está de paso en Macondo. Esto le atribuye un carácter especial de ente sin principio ni fin. No reencarna en otros; reaparece, después de sus falsas muertes y, cuando deja la novela, es porque su función de augur y de escriba está cumplida. Melquíades es sucesivamente y a la vez mago, alquimista, aventurero, experimentador, científico, sabio enciclopédico, mortal, inmortal resucitado y sobre todo y ante todo, viajero que circula libremente por el espacio de la novela y su más allá pasando sin esfuerzo de un mundo a otro, como vínculo y mensajero entre vivos y muertos.»[27] Gullón provides convincing evidence for their similarities, but the narrative voice is not that of Melquíades for several reasons. Melquíades participates in the daily life of the Buendías, but his role is internal in spite of his myriad functions and ubiquity. His power does not extend beyond the confines of the text in the sense that he provides the «telling» which the reader performs. The narrator is omnipresent whereas Melquíades can be situated within the framework of the novel, however intermittent these moments may be. The narrator's voice is uniform and controls the tone and rhythm of the novel from beginning to end. That Melquíades is a narrative persona of García Márquez is probably a more accurate appraisal of the relationship between the two. By virtue of Melquíades' own qualities, he more closely resembles the narrator but in no way assumes any narrative role. The problem remains of how to characterize the narrator.

Gullón describes him as «alguien ajeno a lo narrado, que sabe de los sucesos cuanto hay que saber y los refiere como cronista, sin comentarlos, imperturbable e imperturbado, sin formular juicios morales, ni de otro tipo, sobre lo ocurrido. No pone los hechos en tela de juicio, para él no hay diferencia entre lo verosímil y lo inverosímil; se atiene a su misión—o función—de contarlo todo y habla de los vivos como de los muertos, asociando sin pestañear el fantasma con lo tangible. Su imperturbabilidad se revela en lo inalterable del tono; desde la primera página hasta la última se mantiene al mismo nivel, sin fluctuaciones, sin variantes.»[28] Patricia Tobin characterizes the narrator as «neutral, unobtrusive, steadfast, monochromatic, calm—manifesting qualities we usually associate with the 'middle-distance' narrator in the novel of epic realism. The narrator of *One Hundred Years of Solitude* never exercises the decisive selectivity that follows upon the inevitable distinctions discovered by conceptualized thinking: instead, without comment and without missing a beat, he narrates the mingling of prodigious and miraculous happenings with village and household events within this heterogeneous reality, exuding an equanimity that betrays not irony nor compassion nor humor. Thus the narrator is detached from what he narrates by means of the cool understatement of his voice, yet at the same time he is *with* the characters of the novel because he thinks like them.»[29] These descriptions portray the narrator as both detached yet friendly, omniscient yet noncommittal, omnipresent yet unobtrusive. His omniscience differs from that of the objective narrator of much realistic fiction, for he lacks the control of his fictional world. He displays a singular refusal, or inability, to «make sense» of the unfolding reality of his narrative, yet the reader does not lack confidence in him.

Because he is dealing with a written text, the reader will assume a relationship, either implicit or explicit, between the author and the narrator. Franz Stanzel, in his *Narrative Situations in the Novel,* classifies novels according to three narrative categories. In *authorial* narration, «the author emerges by addressing the reader, by commenting on the action, by reflections, etc., [and] the reader will bridge the gap between his own world and fictional reality under the guidance, so to speak, of the author.»[30] In *figural* narration, «the reader has the illusion of being present on the scene in one of the figures.»[31] The narration is *neutral* if «the point of observation does not lie in any of the novel's figures, although the perspective gives the reader the feeling of being present as an imaginary witness of the events.»[32] Although it is difficult to provide an overall model for the reader's attitude toward *CAS,* these classifications provide some indications. While neither *authorial* nor *figural* narration fits the reader's relationship to the author or narrator, the *neutral* narration describes it more exactly. The narrator in *CAS* thinks like the characters who accept «all things at the level of their conglomerate coexistence.»[33] This neutrality resembles Roland Barthes's idea of the «zero degree of writing» in reverse. When Barthes introduced this concept, he referred specifically to Albert Camus's *The Stranger,* in which Camus had created a language detached from any outside sociological or political context. The impersonal quality of the narrative, and the use of the first person in *The Stranger,* alienate and separate the reader from the narrator.

The use of the zero degree of writing in *CAS* produces a different result. No attempt is made to alienate the reader, and the narrator, by his noncommittal stance, treats the reader as an equal partner in the narrative process. The reader shares the same banality and mystery as the characters, but the fact that he does not understand in no way separates him from either the narrator or the characters. He can be witness or participant, for he has the option of interrupting his reading, but every effort is made to make him an active participant. The lack of sharp distinctions between the narrator, characters and reader signifies that narration, actions and reading become mirror images of the same process which could be subsumed under «telling.» Telling in *CAS* is an eminently *bricolage* process, for it has no other objective than recounting a good story. It is both a continuous and an indeterminate process, for neither the characters, nor the narrator, nor the reader can determine what the final outcome will be.

The narrator is limited by the elements which constitute the history of the Buendía family. All this has been set down first in Sanskrit, and then in Spanish, and his task is to organize it into some kind of narrative. He has already examined all the heterogeneous elements of his narrative repertoire, and he includes all the necessary material from the previous works and does not eliminate it either for the sake of efficiency or for the purpose of a specific project. His refusal to judge, comment, or explain his choices and arrangements indicates that his only project is to tell a good story. He never attempts to go beyond the limits imposed by his material. The «message,» which the narrator transmits in his version of the story of the Buendías, is already contained in the overall myth of Macondo, and the incorporation, deletion and addition of elements do not alter it in any basic way. The narrator refuses to make the same distinctions as science which, as Lévi-Strauss states, distinguishes between event and structure: «The qualities it claimed at its outset as peculiarly scientific were precisely those which formed no part of the living experience and remained outside and, as it were, unrelated to events.»[34] The narrator, unlike the scientist, recounts his events as part of living experience. He injects himself into his narration, puts himself on the same level as his characters, and the reader participates equally in the same living experience.

Instead of emphasizing *what* is narrated, *CAS* focuses on *how* this *what* is narrated; that is, García Márquez was able «to people his novel with characters and, especially a narrator, who have no volition or capacity for knowledge, as traditionally understood by the Western world. Absent from this novel are the articles of faith that stand prior to all historical and scientific pursuits of knowledge: the confidence that 'things add up,' that the singular and discrete element is always part of a larger, knowable totality of order, that the apparently random is inevitably calculable.»[35] If *what* and *why* are replaced by *how* the story is narrated, the reader's position is changed, and he either rejects or accepts this feast of narration, whose ultimate purpose cannot be completely ascertained. The presence of alchemy in the novel serves as both a miniaturized version of the *bricolage* narrative and as a symbol of the opposition to the traditional function of narration in realistic fiction. Patricia Tobin explains that «in his motivation, purpose, and use of materials, Márquez seems peculiarly akin to the alchemist. The medieval Churchmen were not fooled by the alchemists' protestations that they were merely continuing and extending God's work in the world. They knew that a declaration of independence lay behind each mad, inspired experiment; and the alchemists themselves believed that their transforming power depended upon their will and desire to remake the world, to bring to life and clarity all that was dead and opaque in it. Theirs was a rival creation, in competition with the Father. Their central project was to obtain, by opening up a single substance, two opposing materials, which were then analyzed, and finally forced to cooperate or interact within a new and higher substance.»[36] She describes the alchemist, as well as García Márquez, as «a maker who brings forth a unity, out of diverse opposites, through transformations.»[37] In *CAS,* alchemy symbolizes this fusion of telling and writing and the restoration of mythical storytelling. The narrator fulfills this function by emphasizing the «telling» of his story over the *what* and *why* it is told, and he eschews all the traditional prerogatives of the third person, omniscient narrator in favor of the pure joy of telling a story. Although the narrator is limited by certain literary conventions, he uses them in an original way.

In his article entitled «Oral Literature,» Robert Kellogg suggests three general types of literature: «In theory, therefore, we have three possibilities: literature dominated to such an extent by the book that the human voice of the narrator or speaker is silenced; literature with a strong sense both of writing authors and of speaking or narrating voices; and literature consisting entirely of the voices of performers independent of books or authors.»[38] *CAS* lies midway between the second and third possibilities. The narrator's voice is stronger than that of the author, whose presence is more implicit than explicit, more assumed than actually experienced by the reader. The central question is whether this narrative voice, embedded in a written text, uses techniques more appropriate to telling than to writing. This question can be answered by studying the use of the preterite, imperfect, conditional, «haber de,» embedding, enumeration, hyperbole, succession, transformation and the *bricolage* arrangement of events in *CAS*.

Except for the use of the present tense in monologues and dialogues, the preterite, imperfect and conditional dominate in that order. In *CAS,* events have already taken place, and the narrator retells them in absolute terms. Roland Barthes, in *Writing Degree Zero.* explains that the function of the preterite is

> to reduce reality to a point in time, and to abstract, from the depth of a multiplicity of experience, a pure verbal act, freed from the existential roots of knowledge, and directed towards a logical link with other acts, other processes, a general movement of the world; it aims at maintaining a hierarchy in the realm of facts. Through the preterite, the verb implicitly belongs with a causal chain, it partakes of a set of related and oriented actions, it functions as the algebraic sign of an intention. Allowing as it does an ambiguity between temporality and causality, it calls for a sequence of events, that is, for an intelligible Narrative. That is why it is the ideal instrument for every construction of a world; it is the unreal time of cosmogonies, myths, History and Novels. It presupposes a world which is constructed, elaborated, self-sufficient, reduced to significant lines, and not one which has been sent sprawling before us, for us to take or leave. Behind the preterite there always lurks a demiurge, a God or reciter. The world is not unexplained since it is told like a story; each one of its accidents is but a circumstance, and the preterite is precisely this operative sign whereby the narrator reduces the exploded reality to a slim and pure logos, without density, without volume, without spread, and whose sole function is to unite as rapidly as possible a cause and an end."

Although the preterite in *CAS* seems to fit Barthes' notion as the ideal tense for narrating myth and other traditional tales, problems arise immediately. The opening sentences, in which the preterite should reduce the world to familiar terms, instead initiate a series of events which explode into disarray. The first preterite action occurs when Colonel Aureliano Buendía's father took him to discover ice. This preterite action is not completed until the end of the chapter. The next one occurs when the gypsies brought the magnet. Again the causal relationship breaks down, and it unleashes a series of uncoordinated actions. Finally, to complete the illogical sequence, José Arcadio Buendía «pensó que era posible servirse de aquella invención inútil para desentrañar el oro de la tierra» (p. 9). Melquíades tries to restore the logic inherent in the preterite tense (le previno: «Para esto no sirve»), but this is useless. The narrator either contradicts the logic of the preterite or uses it to narrate illogically. After composing a manual on solar warfare based on the use of the magnifying glass, José Arcadio Buendía sent a messenger «que atravesó la sierra, se extravió en pantanos desmesurados, remontó ríos tormentosos y estuvo a punto de perecer bajo el azote de las fieras, la desesperación y la peste, antes de conseguir una ruta de enlace con las mulas del correo» (p. 11). This illogical process is repeated again and again, and the preterite loses its rational function and allies itself with the simple function of telling.

The preterite is usually associated with what Patricia Tobin calls patrilineal narration:

> Within the extended family the individual member is guaranteed both identity and legitimacy through the tracing of his lineage back to the founding father, the family's origin and first cause. This project-in-retrospect of the children is matched in the prospective design of the father. He extends the paternal promise of purpose throughout his progeny, bestowing upon them a legacy that contains within this structural unity an entire history of meaning. By an analogy of function, events in time come to be perceived as begetting other events within a line of causality similar to the line of generations, with the prior event earning a special prestige as it is seen to originate, control, and predict future events. The same lineal decorum pervades the structure of realistic narrative: all possibly random events and gratuitous details are brought into an alignment of relevance, so that at the point of conclusion all possibility has been converted into necessity within a line of kinship—the subsequent having been referred to the prior, the end to the beginning, the progeny to the father.[10]

The preterite fulfills this function by emphasizing how things happened, but in *CAS,* García Márquez reverses it, and assigns to it the simple task of telling. The progeny of the preterite in *CAS* are illegitimate, verbal children who no longer obey the genealogical imperative imposed by father preterite.

The revolt against the preterite is evident during the insomnia plague whose primary symptom is that everyone starts to forget. In order to combat the disease, Ursula «preparó e hizo beber a todos un brebaje de acónito, pero no consiguieron dormir, sino que estuvieron todo el día soñando despiertos» (p. 45). Here the preterite not only narrates what happened, but its inherent logic is undermined by the narrative sequence. The logic inherent in «preparó» leads to the opposite effect, but the important point is that how it happened is deleted. Not only does the preterite fail in its patrilineal function, but the patriarchal lineage of the Buendías also fails to combat the plague. José Arcadio Buendía, the patriarch, actually contributes to the spread of the plague when his little caramel animals continue to be sold in Macondo «de modo que el alba del lunes sorprendió despierto a todo el pueblo» (p. 45). The addition of «no se perdonó jamás» for his carelessness underlines the subversion of the preterite. The Buendía men all proceed by chance in combatting the plague. Aureliano starts writing down the names of everything, but «no se le ocurrió que fuera aquella la primera manifestación del olvido, porque el objeto tenía un nombre difícil de recordar» (p. 47). The Buendía men try to recapture the genealogical imperative, but their efforts, like the preterite, are singularly futile. The inhabitants «continuaron viviendo en una realidad escurridiza, momentáneamente capturada por las palabras, pero que había de fugarse sin remedio cuando olvidaran los valores de la letra escrita» (p. 47). In an attempt to combat the plague and the loss of memory, the Buendía men turn to science in order to solve their problem. The loss of memory would spell the end of the preterite, because it would no longer have anything to narrate. The patrilineal imperative fails again because writing down all the words proves so cumbersome that «Pilar Ternera fue quien más contribuyó a popularizar esa manifestación, cuando concibió el artificio de leer el pasado en las barajas como antes había leído el futuro» (p. 48). As Barthes says, the preterite «is the very act by which society affirms its possession of its past and its possibility.»[41] In CAS, reading cards replaces the power of the preterite and undermines its ability to record the past, and in the end, the preterite chronicles its own demise by telling what happened. Melquíades «le dio a beber a José Arcadio Buendía una sustancia de color apacible, y la luz se hizo en su memoria. Los hojos se la humedecieron de llanto, antes de verse a sí mismo en una sala absurda donde los objetos estaban marcados, y antes de avergonzarse de las solemnes tonterías escritas en las paredes, y aun antes de reconocer el recién llegado en un deslumbrante resplandor de alegría. Era Melquíades» (p. 49). Magic, not logic, solves (or cures) the malady of forgetfulness, and this passage provides a comic image of the preterite denuded of its logical function in the person of the patriarch of the whole Buendía lineage. The preterite is not superior to other verb tenses, and the narrator divests it of its supposed powers to order the past chronologically and thereby implicitly predict the future. The paradox is that everything is already known, so the preterite should enjoy a privileged status in this narration. As Patricia Tobin says: «Traditionally, the narrator of a novel is telling us either what has happened or what he has remembered, and we are accustomed to assume, as with historical narratives, that the business of 'knowing' the past is largely a matter of assigning plausible cause-effect relations among established facts. With this conversion of the past to a visionary future where all is guessed, we are confronted with the probability that our unobtrusive narrator has taken things so calmly because he is one incarnation of the gypsy Melquíades, to whom 'everything is known.'»[42] The narrator should therefore use the preterite to communicate *what* and *how* things happened, but instead he leaves out *how* and *why* things have taken place, and violates the traditional narrative imperatives of the preterite.

This subversion of verb tenses also extends to the use of the imperfect. The imperfect usually deals with states (natural, psychological, physical, etc.) which reinforce the preterite by providing an explanatory dimension and expanding the potentially denuded reality communicated by the preterite. In *CAS,* however, the imperfect is incorporated into the telling process, loses its static quality, and becomes part of the rapid narrative pace, and the reader rarely has time to stop and consider its possible implications. Instead of elucidating the motivations of the characters' actions, the narrator in *CAS* uses the imperfect to advance the flow of his narration, and its static, atemporal quality is lost. Even when the imperfect appears to fulfill its traditional function, it remains unclear because the explanation it provides may belong to another event not yet narrated. Both the preterite and the imperfect are part of the process of «deslizamiento insensible» whereby the narrator glides from one event to another, one character to another, or one action to another without the slightest interruption in the narrative current.[43] For example, when Melquíades says the magnet is not used for the purpose of unearthing gold, the only answer given is «pero José Arcadio Buendía no creía en aquel tiempo en la honradez de los gitanos, así que cambió su mulo y una partida de chivos por los dos lingotes imantados» (p. 9). The narrator uses temporal notations such as «en aquel tiempo» to either situate the preterite action or imperfect explanation, or to place them in a projected time period, or to link different time periods. The narrator tells *what* José Arcadio Buendía believed at the time, but neither *how* nor *why* he did not believe in the honor of gypsies. The narrator also reveals that José Arcadio Buendía's «desaforada imaginación iba siempre más lejos que el ingenio de la naturaleza y aun más allá del milagro y la magia» (p. 9), but no explanation is given. This notation of the state of José Arcadio Buendía's imagination does, however, anticipate many of his later actions. The imperfect, which is also used to recount habitual actions in the past, generates other actions produced by each return of the gypsies, but their successive visits are never explained. The imperfect provides the narrator with an excellent tool to produce more events in the preterite, and to anticipate the future states of characters without explaining them.

A related use is made of the paraphrases with the verb «haber de,» and the temporal indications like «muchos años después.» The frequent use of «haber de» permits the narrator to summarize the different reactions of the characters, and it is often used with the verbs «recordar» and «acordarse.» Nila Gutiérrez Marrone explains that the use of «haber de» «es una especie de *leitmotif* a través de la obra, con la que se introduce escenas del pasado. 'Haber de' es una construcción de significación obligativa que ha caído en desuso en el lenguaje hablado, pero que nuestras abuelas usaban mucho, de ahí que tiene un especial sabor a lo añejo. Su utilización como primer verbo de la novela recuerda la fórmula narrativa del comienzo de cuentos fantásticos o fábulas 'Dice que había una vez,' y establece el mismo tono narrativo fabuloso que se irá confirmando a través de la obra. Gili Gaya indica que 'haber de' es la perífrasis verbal obligativa más antigua.»" «Haber de» is often employed when an event is projected into the past, or future, and this depersonalizes the event by removing it from the immediate narrative flow: «Años después, frente al pelotón de fusilamiento, Arcadio había de acordarse del temblor con que Melquíades le hizo escuchar varias páginas de su escritura impenetrable, que por supuesto no entendió, pero que al ser leídas en voz alta parecían encíclicas cantadas» (p. 68). This passage refers to a past event and to the future obsession of the Arcadios with the parchments. And later: «Pocos meses después, frente al pelotón de fusilamiento, Arcadio había de revivir los pasos perdidos en el salón de clase, los tropiezos contra los escaños, y por último la densidad de un cuerpo en las tinieblas del cuarto y los latidos del aire bombeado por un corazón que no era el suyo» (p. 101). «Haber de» used in the imperfect thus allows the narrator to incorporate various static states within the flow of the narration without lengthy explanations. The use of formulas such as «muchos años después» functions in a similar way. They would not be out of place if they were governed by chronology, but the novel lacks any precise dates. Their primary function is to order events in the particular way in which the narrator wishes without any preconceived, chronological system. The Colonel's execution demonstrates this technique. The narrator uses these temporal references to diminish the reader's distance from the event until the moment in which the event actually takes place (pp. 9, 21, 50, 68, 75, 82, 87 and 94).

The limited use of the conditional serves as a kind of prophetic future, for it refers to the future from a past context. Roberto Gullón calls the narrator of *CAS* a «profeta-cronista» who «ha visto lo porvenir (si acaso no lo ha vivido en otra vuelta de la rueda), y lo anticipa en su historia.»[45] The conditional, like the future, has its own uncertain predictability. Tzvetan Todorov, analyzing the prophetic future in the *Odyssey,* discerns several subdivisions: «First from the viewpoint of the state or attitude of the author of the speech-act. Sometimes it is the gods who speak in the future. This future is then not a supposition, but a certitude: what they predict will occur. Thus Circe, or Calypso, or Athena predicts to Odysseus what will happen to him. Alongside this divine future, there is the divinatory future of men—men trying to read the signs sent by the gods. Another range of subdivisions is to be found in the relations of the future tense with the instance of discourse. The future which will come about in the course of the pages that follow is only one of these types: let us call it the prospective future. Alongside it exists the retrospective future, in which we are told an event while also being told or reminded that it had been foretold.»[46] The use of «haber de» sometimes fulfills the function of the prospective future. For example, when Melquíades, «como una prueba de su admiración le hizo un regalo que había de ejercer una influencia terminante en el futuro de la aldea: un laboratorio de alquimia» (p. 12). In spite of Ursula's orientation towards reality, the smell of the cinnabar «quedaría para siempre en su memoria, vinculado al recuerdo de Melquíades» (p. 13). The restricted use of the conditional in *CAS* reveals the non-judgmental stance of the narrator whose predictive powers are as limited as those of the characters, and he undertakes the same voyage of discovery. His position resembles that of the adventurer and the teller in the *Odyssey:* «There are two Odysseuses in the *Odyssey:* one has the adventures, the other tells them. It is difficult to say which of the two is the main character. Athena herself is in some doubt: 'Poor eternal storyteller! All your hunger is for ruses...You return to your country and still you think only of robbers' tales and the lies dear to your heart since childhood.' If Odysseus takes so long to return home, it is because home is not his deepest desire: his desire is that of the narrator (who is telling Odysseus' lies, Odysseus or Homer?). But the narrator desires to tell. Odysseus resists returning to Ithaca so that the story can continue. The theme of the *Odyssey* is not Odysseus' return to Ithaca; this return is, on the contrary, the death of the *Odyssey,* its end. The theme of the *Odyssey* is the narrative forming the *Odyssey,* it is the *Odyssey* itself. This is why, returning home, Odysseus does not think about it, does not rejoice over it; he thinks only of 'robbers' tales and lies'—he thinks the *Odyssey.*»[47] The verb tenses in *CAS* communicate the same idea as expressed by Todorov concerning the *Odyssey.* The narrator will disappear with the conclusion of his narrative, but his narrative task allows him to prolong it as long as possible.

The desire to narrate communicated by the verb tenses brings up an important idea related to the telling process of *CAS:* embedding. Discussing works like the *Arabian Nights,* Todorov states that «they lack internal analysis of the characters, that there is no description of the psychological states. Psychological narrative regards each action as a means of access to the personality in question, as an expression if not a symptom. Action is not considered in itself, it is *transitive* with regard to its subject. A-psychological narrative, on the contrary, is characterized by intransitive actions; action is important in itself and not as an indication of this or that character trait. The *Arabian Nights* derive, we might say, from *predicative* literature: the emphasis will always fall on the predicate and not on the subject of the proposition.»[48] He goes on to say that «the *Arabian Nights* belong to the realm of common sense (of folklore), and the abundance of examples suffices to convince us that we are not concerned here with another psychology, nor even with an antipsychology, but with a-psychology.»[49] The primary method of communicating this a-psychology is what Todorov calls embedding: «The appearance of a new character invariably involves the interruption of the preceding story, so that a new story, the one which explains 'now I am here' of the new character, may be told to us. A second story is enclosed within the first; this device is called *embedding.*»[50]

Embedding is an essential component in *CAS.* In the first chapter, the successive visits of the gypsies assure the continuation of the narration through embedding. The opening sentence is also an example of embedding which insures the Colonel's existence. He will discover ice at the end of the first chapter, but his experience before the firing squad and all the related events will come later. When the gypsies arrive the first time, José Arcadio Buendía unleashes his unbridled imagination. This not only serves as a basis for stories within the chapter, but also for his other actions and those of his descendants. Each return of the gypsies, implanted at the beginning, involves a variation of the initial story and opens the way to future ones. Each time Ursula opposes these flights of imagination, she sets in motion a series of actions which will typify the female members of the Buendía clan. Even the discovery of ice by Aureliano Buendía opens the way to the «ciudad de los espejos» which culminates in the founding of Macondo. Melquíades' death serves as a paradigm for all the deaths, and the dead either fade away or return to haunt the Buendías. The first chapter thus demonstrates this embedding process which will take place throughout the novel. As Todorov says of the *Arabian Nights,* «the first narrative (like the first chapter of *CAS)* subdivides and multiplies into a thousand and one nights of narratives. Each narrative seems to have something excessive, a supplement which remains outside the closed form produced by the development of the plot. At the same time, and for this very reason, this something-more, proper to the narrative, is also something-less. This supplement is also a lack; in order to supply this lack created by the supplement, another narrative is necessary.»[51] In *CAS,* the narration of each arrival of the gypsies also represents a lack. The narrator, despite his omniscience, has chosen to narrate his material from a viewpoint which restricts his global knowledge, and obliges him to participate in the unfolding story. Embedding becomes his primary means of discovering the final outcome of his narration, and each end is another beginning. To start is to finish in a continuous fashion, for the reader, as well as the narrator.

The shift in narrative styles from *H* to *FMG* coincides with the introduction of enumeration and hyperbole which abound in *CAS.* Enumeration, as Patricia Tobin explains, is «Western man's expression of faith in knowledge as the establishment of an orderly succession of things. Any series or sequence is built upon inference: in reference to the beginning term (the father), each successive member of the series (his progeny) becomes increasingly predictive until the completion of the series, when certainty is reached and the connections have become inevitable.»[52] In *CAS,* «the long enumerations are deprived of this logic because the identity of their parts has not been established with reference to the differences among the 'family' of things. When, within enumeration, everything is equally present in a kinship of undifferentiated aggregation, then the paternal promise of order becomes a farce, and the 'family line' of language is exposed as an illegitimate, heterogeneous community of unruly orphans.»[53] Enumerations of this type are found throughout *CAS*. When José Arcadio Buendía sends his plans for solar warfare to the capital, the messenger «atravesó la sierra, se extravió en pantanos desmesurados, remontó ríos tormentosos y estuvo a punto de perecer bajo el azote de las fieras, la desesperación y la peste, antes de conseguir una ruta de enlace con las mulas del correo» (p. 11). The narrator simply adds that «a pesar de que el viaje a la capital era en aquel tiempo poco menos que imposible, José Arcadio Buendía prometía intentarlo tan pronto como se lo ordenara el gobierno» (p. 11). After receiving some navigational instruments from Melquíades, he decided to «abrir una trocha que pusiera a Macondo en contacto con los grandes inventos» (p. 16), though he was totally ignorant of the region's geogrpahy. His trip is nothing but an illogical enumeration of random movements which ends in failure at the edge of the sea, and he concludes that Macondo is surrounded by water on all sides.

García Márquez uses hyperbole to accentuate the absurdity of the enumerations, and to subvert their logic. He often mixes the daily and the marvelous in the same enumeration. When Remedios, la bella, disappears into the heavens, the daily and marvelous intermingle: «Acabó de decirlo, cuando Fernanda sintió que un delicado viento de luz le arrancó las sábanas de las manos y las desplegó en toda su amplitud. Amaranta sintió un temblor misterioso en los encajes de sus pollerinas y trató de agarrarse de la sábana para no caer, en el instante en que Remedios, la bella, empezaba a elevarse» (p. 205). Sheets, delicate winds of light, and mysterious tremblings are all combined to produce an aggregation of heterogeneous elements of equal value. The enumeration of the Colonel's exploits offers one of the most complete combinations of hyperbolic enumerations in which logic is negated at each step: «El coronel Aureliano Buendía promovió treinta y dos levantamientos armados y los perdió todos. Tuvo diecisiete hijos varones de diecisiete mujeres distintas, que fueron exterminados uno tras otro en una sola noche, antes de que el mayor cumpliera treinta y cinco años. Escapó a catorce atentados, a setenta y tres emboscados y a un pelotón de fusilamiento» (p. 94). This enumeration is revealing not only because the logic of his actions is denied, but the numbers assume hyperbolic dimensions, rendering the enumeration all the more incredible. Numbers usually serve to mark the repeated, meaningful efforts made by someone, but the Colonel's actions, like those of many Buendía characters, are singularly purposeless. In *CAS,* enumeration restores the heterogeneous quality of reality, and the reader is forced to confront the mass of conglomerate reality. The narrator tells, enumerates, and records reality, but the fact that everything is equal produces its own hyperbolic quality.

Todorov classifies narratives according to certain categories: gnoseological, ideological and mythological.[54] In the first two cases, «transformations acquire predominance over succession because they contribute to a search for knowledge, the emphasis now shifted from the event itself to the correct or incorrect perception of the event.»[55] In mythological narrative, «the structure...unfolds under the two principles of succession and transformation, but heavily favors the former. Succession develops its action from a series of discontinuous events whose units are put into relation on this one level, whereas transformation makes visible the paradigm for all change, whereby one term is converted into its opposite or contradictory one»[56] In *CAS,* the narrator favors succession over transformation, and the result is a narrative composed of discontinuously and successively connected events. The first chapter serves as a paradigm for this process, and it can be argued that García Márquez placed this chapter first to accustom the reader to this process. The second chapter, with its account of the predecessors of the Buendía lineage, is the novel's logical starting point. The first chapter, opening with two discontinuous and successively linked events, surprises the reader, and the successive returns of the gypsies do nothing to alleviate his predicament. As Tobin says, for the reader «deprived of the binary logic of the father, events lose their certification of legitimacy and become the bastards of process.»[57] García Márquez is collapsing «the metaphorical axis of language, leaving the figurative and symbolic, undistinguished from the literal sign, afloat within the same single, metonymical stream.»[58] The narrator in *CAS* generates a linear flow, but refuses to control it, or to provide the reader with any sense of preconceived order.

The narrator's posture in *CAS* is akin to the *bricoleur* who confronts a particular project. The principle of succession also dominates his approach to his project, so that he produces a structure whose components are constantly subject to reordering. Transformation implies that the narrator, or *bricoleur,* attempts to transcend the inherent limitations of his materials and to transmit what is not part of his materials. The narrator of *CAS,* limited by the events comprising the history of the Buendías, narrates them without alteration, respecting the proviso that they were arranged so as to coexist in an instant. Succession means that the final outcome cannot be known beforehand, because reality does not unfold according to a predetermined pattern. The first chapter initiates the reader into this *bricolage* universe because the narrator opens so many narrative lines that the reader cannot know the final outcome until he reads the entire novel. Reading itself becomes a form of intellectual *bricolage,* and the termination of the novel only marks the end of a step in the telling of the story. *CAS* supplements and completes certain aspects of García Márquez' fictional world, but because of succession, there is still much left unexplained at the end when everything vanishes without a trace.

CAS is a symbiotic compromise between a telling and a writing. The narrative and narrator combine elements appropriate to oral and written literature to produce a text which can be read (and told perhaps) with equal ease. *CAS* shifts the emphasis from writing to telling, restores the importance of the spoken word. Pure oral literature may be a lost art in our society since the written word has assumed a disproportionate value in relation to what is transmitted orally. *CAS* revolts against the written word by telling a story whose content forces the reader to re-evaluate his own requirements for knowledge. Its revolutionary quality is precisely that this story can be transmitted on many levels without recourse to a narrative which explains everything.

NOTES

1.   Robert Kellogg, «Oral Literature,» *New Literary History,* Vol. V, No. I (Autumn, 1973), p. 55.

2.   Robert Scholes and Robert Kellogg, *The Nature of Narrative* (New York: Oxford University Press, 1966), pp. 18-19.

3.   Kellogg, p. 57.

4.   *Ibid.,* p. 57.

5.   *Ibid.,* p. 58.

6.   Dennis Tedlock, «Toward an Oral Poetics,» *New Literary History,* Vol. VIII, No. 3 (Spring, 1977), p. 509.

7.   Italo Calvino, «Myth in the Narrative,» in: *Surfiction: Fiction Now...and Tomorrow* (Chicago: The Swallow Press, 1975), p. 77.

8.   Harald Weinrich, «Structures narratives du mythe,» *Poétique, I (1970), pp. 25-6.*

9.   *Ibid.,* p. 25. The translation is mine.

10.   Mircea Eliade, *Myth and Reality,* trans. Willard R. Trask (New York: Harper & Row, 1963), pp. 5-6.

11. Northrup Frye, *Anatomy of Criticism* (Princeton: Princeton University Press, 1957), p. 366.

12. Northrup Frye, *Fables of Identity: Studies in Poetic Mythology* (New York: Harcourt, Brace & World, Inc., 1963), p. 31.

13. Kellogg, p. 58.

14. Scholes and Kellogg, pp. 272-3.

15. *Ibid.*, pp. 265-66.

16. Claude Lévi-Strauss, *The Savage Mind* (Chicago: The University of Chicago Press, 1970), p. 17.

17. *Ibid.*, p. 17.

18. *Ibid.*, p. 19.

19. *Ibid.*, p. 21.

20. *Ibid.*, p. 21.

21. *Ibid.*, p. 21.

22. Roger Fowler, *Linguistics and the Novel* (London: Methuen & Co., Ltd., 1977), pp. 89-90.

23. *Ibid.*, p. 75.

24. Ricardo Gullón, *García Márquez o el olvidado arte de contar* (Madrid: Taurus Ediciones, S. A., 1970), p. 22.

25. *Ibid.*, p. 22.

26. *Ibid.*, pp. 22-3.

27. *Ibid.*, p. 23.

28. *Ibid.*, p. 19.

29. Patricia Drechsel Tobin, *Time and the Novel: The Genealogical Imperative* (Princeton: Princeton University Press, 1978), pp. 171-2.

30. Franz Stanzel, *Narrative Situations in the Novel,* trans. James P. Pusack (Bloomington: Indiana University Press, 1971), p. 23.

31. *Ibid.*, p. 23.

32. *Ibid.*, p. 23.

33. Tobin, p. 172.

34. Lévi-Strauss, *The Savage Mind,* p. 21.

35. Tobin, p. 168.

36. *Ibid.*, pp. 175-6.

37. *Ibid.*, p. 176.

38. Kellogg, p. 57.

39. Roland Barthes, *Writing Degree Zero,* trans. Annette Lavers and Colin Smith (Boston: Beacon Press, 1970), pp. 30-1.

40. Tobin, pp. 7-8.

41. Barthes, p. 33.

42. Tobin, p. 177.

43. José Miguel Oviedo, Hugo Achugar and Jorge Arbeleche, *Aproximación a Gabriel García Márquez* (Montevideo: Fundación de Cultura Universitaria, 1969),

p. 30.

44. Nila Gutiérrez Marrone, *El estilo de Juan Rulfo: estudio lingüístico* (New York: Bilingual Press, 1978), pp. 18-19.

45. Gullón, p. 22.

46. Tzvetan Todorov, *The Poetics of Prose,* trans. Richard Howard (Ithaca: Cornell University Press, 1977), pp. 63-4.

47. *Ibid.,* pp. 62-3.

48. *Ibid.,* pp. 67.

49. *Ibid.,* p. 69.

50. *Ibid.,* p. 70.

51. *Ibid.,* p. 76.

52. Tobin, p. 178.

53. *Ibid.,* p. 178.

54. *Ibid.,* p. 173-4.

55. *Ibid.,* p. 174.

56. *Ibid.,* p. 174.

57. *Ibid.,* p. 175.

58. *Ibid.,* p. 174.

THE MYTHICAL FAMILY, CHARACTERS AND *BRICOLAGE* IN *CIEN AÑOS DE SOLEDAD*

CHAPTER 6

In the three previous chapters, *CAS*'s mythical structure and the narrator as a storyteller of myth have been examined, and attention can now be focused on the gross constituents of the myth of Macondo. Myth, according to Lévi-Strauss, is composed of bundles of mythemes or gross constituent units which function on a supra-linguistic level. They are derived from a comparison of all the variants of a myth, and they constitute the message, or code, which is transmitted intact from version to version. In *CAS,* one of the gross constituents is the family. Within the overall structure of the Buendía clan, there exist matriarchal and patriarchal divisions. Given the endogamic patterns within the family, the Oedipus myth and incest play important roles. Certain characters, Ursula Iguarán, José Arcadio Buendía, Colonel Aureliano Buendía and Melquíades, overshadow the others and must be considered separately. An analysis of these aspects will provide a comprehensive view of the mythic structure of the Buendía family.

The importance of the family is already evident in *H* and *FMG.* In *H,* the three different narrators represent three generations who produce a fragmentary picture of the family. People came to Macondo towards the end of the 19th century to escape the civil wars, and there they found a place in which adherence to family traditions dominated. The Colonel's family lived in feudal splendor before the ravages of the civil war, and upon arriving in Macondo, they found «el sitio apropiado para reconstruir la casa que pocos años después sería una mansión rural, con tres caballerizas y dos cuartos para los huéspedes» (p. 39). The founding families represent the aristocratic class in Macondo, and they are tradition-bound, hard working, and closely tied to the earth. Isabel's father, the Colonel, «venía dispuesto a echar raíces contra viento y marea» (p. 40). After the death of his first wife, he marries a woman named Adelaida whose meticulous manners reveal that she belongs to the insiders in Macondo. The Colonel's family also welcomes many outsiders into its house, but they do not belong to Macondo's inner social structure. The doctor lived in the Colonel's house for eight years, and, in spite of the town's hatred for him, the Colonel promises to fulfill his duty to bury him. His sense of duty reflects the importance of tradition for the founding families. If the Colonel's family easily accommodates outsiders, it is impossible for it to incorporate the incursion of progress which undermines the traditional structure of Macondo to such an extent that the natives become the outsiders. There is also a strong link between the generations. The Colonel's family carried with it «los baúles llenos con la ropa de los muertos anteriores al nacimiento de ellos mismos, de los antepasados que no podrían encontrarse a veinte brazas bajo la tierra» (p. 39). The distant relatives of the Colonel's family «eran primos hermanos entre sí» (p. 39). This detail introduces the idea of endogamic relations which will govern the family structure in *CAS*. The references to Colonel Aureliano Buendía anticipate his inclusion in the Buendía family in *CAS*. The family in *H* represents the most important social unit, and it is not only deeply rooted in Macondo's soil, but also in the past. It is a patriarchal family dominated by the Colonel. Tradition, and a strong sense of succession of generations characterize the family, and the reference to the endogamic relationships of the Colonel's remote ancestors reflects the insulated nature of the family.

In *FMG*, the matriarchal domination of the family is much less organized, and endogamic relations govern the clan: «La rigidez matriarcal de la Mamá Grande había cercado su fortuna y su apellido con una alambrada sacramental, dentro de la cual los tíos se casaban con las hijas de las sobrinas, y los primos con las tías, y los hermanos con las cuñadas, hasta formar una intricada maraña de consaguinidad que convirtió la procreación en un círculo vicioso» (p. 129). Big Mamá's family seems to grow and multiply without any patriarchal input. The «varones habían fecundado hatos, veredas y caseríos con toda una descendencia bastarda, que circulaba entre la servidumbre sin apellidos a título de ahijados, dependientes, favoritos y protegidos de la Mamá Grande» (p. 129). Procreation does not adhere to any lineal idea of generations; rather, it explodes in all directions, creating a wide assortment of people whose classification is determined by their relationship to the official family. Mamá Grande rejects the patriarchal imperative as the governing principle of the family: «La

Mamá Grande, que hasta los cincuenta años rechazó a los más apasionados pretendientes, y que fue dotada por la naturaleza para amamantar ella sola a toda su especie, agonizaba virgen y sin hijos» (p. 133). No one escapes the cohesion of the official family. Magdalena, who tried to leave the family circle, «aterrorizada por las alucinaciones se hizo exorcizar por el padre Antonio Isabel, se rapó la cabeza y renunció a las glorias y vanidades del mundo en el noviciado de la Prefectura Apostólica» (p. 129). Mamá Grande progressively withdraws from any contact with men: «Cada vez más imprecisa y remota, visible apenas en su balcón sofocado entonces por los geranios en las tardes de calor, la Mamá Grande se esfumaba en su propia leyenda» (p. 133). She exercises her authority through Nicanor, who is reducing all the males to ceremonial roles, and her empire is quite the opposite of the patriarchal orderliness in *H:* «Nadie conocía el origen, ni los límites ni el valor real del patrimonio, pero todo el mundo se había acostumbrado a creer que la Mamá Grande era dueña de las aguas corrientes y estancadas, llovidas y por llover, y de los caminos vecinales, los postes del telégrafo, los años bisiestos y el calor, y que tenía además un derecho heredado sobre vida y haciendas» (pp. 129-130). The ubiquitous Colonel Aureliano Buendía is referred to several times, and it is a woman (Mamá Grande's maternal grandmother) who «se enfrentó a una patrulla del coronel Aureliano Buendía, atrincherada en la cocina de la hacienda» (p. 130). Her reign produces incredible confusion and profusion, but she maintains strict control of the internal circle of her family.

The patriarchal family of *H* and the matriarchal one of *FMG* coincide and diverge in several ways. A sense of linear progression and tradition dominates *H,* and power is transmitted from generation to generation through the male members. Isabel says that she does not wish to attend the doctor's funeral, but her father's authority compels her to be present. The weight of the past is much greater in *H.* In both families, a small nucleus, dominated by endogamic relations, constitutes their essence, and endogamy is much more pronounced in *FMG.* The patriarchal family in *H* is more organized, and its static structure opposes the incursions of progress and the foreign elements which accompany it. Patriarchy is equivalent to rigidity, and this same rigidity characterizes Macondo which waxes and wanes with the invasion of progress. In the matriarchal family of *FMG,* the family structure is more flexible, and its system of endogamic relationships spreads its roots to all parts of Mamá Grande's dominion. The matriarchal and patriarchal systems first collide then merge in *CAS* to form a unique family pattern.

It is first necessary to establish the genealogy of the Buendía family. Josefina Ludmer offers the following plan:[1]

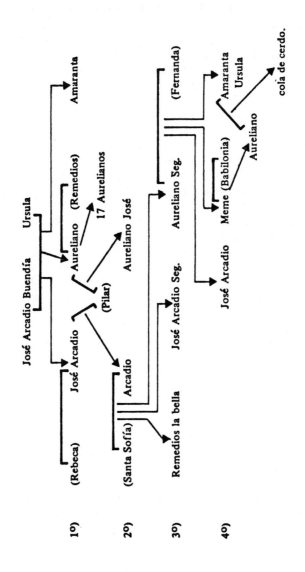

The names in parentheses refer to characters who do not belong to the Buendía clan, but who married or had children by Buendías. The brackets refer to marriages, or sexual unions, and the arrows designate the children of each couple. From the original couple, José Arcadio Buendía and Ursula Iguarán, three children are born: José Arcadio, Aureliano and Amaranta. José Arcadio and Aureliano marry outsiders, Rebeca and Remedios, and Amaranta remains a virgin. Two children, Arcadio and Aureliano José, result from the sexual relationships the two men have with Pila Ternera. Aureliano also produces 17 Aurelianos who all die rather mysteriously. In the second cycle, Arcadio marries Santa Sofía de la Piedad while Aureliano José remains celibate. In the third cycle, Santa Sofía and Arcadio produce three children: Remedios, la bella, and the twins, José Arcadio Segundo and Aureliano Segundo. Neither Remedios nor José Arcadio Segundo marries. Aureliano Segundo marries Fernanda and they have three children: José Arcadio, Meme, and Amaranta Ursula. Meme's relationship with Mauricio Babilonia produces Aureliano. Amaranta Ursula, who married Gastón, eventually forgets about him and engages in incest with Aureliano. From this incestuous union comes the child born with a pig's tail, and this fulfills Ursula's fear.

Vargas Llosa offers another version of the Buendía's lineage which places more emphasis on the succession of generations:

primera) Ursula Iguarán y José Arcadio Buendía:

segunda) José Arcadio el protomacho, el coronel Aureliano Buendía y Amaranta;

tercera) Arcadio (hijo de José Arcadio y Pilar Ternera), Aureliano José (hijo del coronel Buendía y Pilar Ternera), y 17 Aurelianos de la guerra;

cuarta) Remedios la bella, José Arcadio Segundo y Aureliano Segundo;

quinta) José Arcadio el seminarista, Renata Remedios y Amaranta Ursula (todos hijos de Aureliano Segundo y Fernanda del Carpio);

sexta) Aureliano Buendía, quien descifra los manuscritos y

séptima) Aureliano, el niño monstruoso (hijo de Aureliano el sanscritista y de su tía Amaranta Ursula). El último de la estirpe vive apenas unas horas o minutos, antes que lo devoren las hormigas. [2]

Vargas Llosa says that «la historia de la familia, además de estar narrada verticalmente, siguiendo la cronología, lo está horizontalmente: las constantes y variantes que hay de padres a hijos y entre los miembros de cada generación; la vida pública de la familia, expuesta al conocimiento de todos los macondinos, y la vida íntima, oculta por los muros de la casa y que los demás sólo conocen por rumores o ignoran.» [3] He also stresses the patriarchal division of labor within the family: «El rasgo familiar dominante es la inferioridad de la mujer y esta división estricta de funciones perdura los cien años de la estirpe: los varones son los miembros activos y productores, los que trabajan, se enriquecen, guerrean y se lanzan en aventuras descabelladas, en tanto que la función de las mujeres es permanecer en el hogar y ocuparse de las tareas domésticas, como barrer, cocinar, fregar, bordar. El hombre es amo y señor del mundo, la mujer ama y señora del hogar en esta familia de corte feudal.» [4]

Both Ludmer's and Vargas Llosa's family trees stress the idea of successive generations, and the idea of circularity seen in the repetition of names and characteristics inherited by each new generation from the first couple. Every time Ursula tries to give a new arrival a different name, she yields, and the repetitive calamities continue. Even when Amaranta Ursula tries to name her son Rodrigo, her husband objects, saying that «se llamará Aureliano y ganará treinta y dos guerras» (p. 346). The names are an indelible mark of the fate which culminates in the pig's tail. The two family trees do not take into account the Buendías who preceded José Arcadio Buendía and Ursula Iguarán, namely «un comerciante aragonés» and «don José Arcadio Buendía, un criollo cultivador de tabaco» (p. 24). The reader learns that «varios siglos más tarde, el tataranieto del criollo se casó la tataranieta del aragonés» (p. 24). Despite Ursula's fears about marrying José Arcadio Buendía, it was «un simple recurso de desahogo, porque en verdad estaban ligados hasta la muerte por un vínculo más sólido que el amor: un común remordimiento de conciencia. Eran primos entre sí. Habían crecido juntos en la antigua ranchería que los antepasados de ambos transformaron con su trabajo y sus buenas costumbres en uno de los mejores pueblos de la provincia» (pp. 24-5). The endogamic relations and the fear of incest already haunted them before they actually started producing their own lineage. The relatives tried to prevent their marriage because «tenían el temor de que aquellos saludables cabos de dos razas secularmente entrecruzadas pasaran por la vergüenza de engendrar iguanas» (p. 25). This primordial fear and the actual precedent of an uncle of Ursula who had a pig's tail do exist, but this does not stop the lineage from being formed through the endogamic marriage of Ursula and José Arcadio Buendía. The Buendía family's predecessors are important because they establish the theme of incest and the ineluctability of a fate which started long before the actual Buendía clan was formed.

Each new generation inherits the characteristics of José Arcadio Buendía and Ursula Iguarán. José Arcadio Buendía was «el hombre más emprendedor que se veía jamás en la aldea, una especie de patriarca juvenil que daba instrucciones para la siembra y consejos para la crianza de niños y animales, y colaboraba con todos, aun en el trabajo físico, para la buena marcha de la comunidad» (p. 15). But he inevitably lost himself in the excesses of his own imagination which «iba siempre más lejos que el ingenio de la naturaleza, y aun más allá del milagro y la magia» (p. 9). He always remained «ajeno a la existencia de sus hijos, en parte porque consideraba la infancia como un período de insuficiencia mental, y en parte porque siempre estaba demasiado absorto en sus propias especulaciones quiméricas» (p. 21). This division extends to the first two male descendants, Aureliano and José Arcadio: «José Arcadio, el mayor de los niños, había cumplido catorce años. Tenía la cabeza cuadrada, el pelo hirsuto y el carácter voluntarioso de su padre. Aunque llevaba el mismo impulso de crecimiento y fortaleza física, ya desde entonces era evidente que carecía de imaginación. Fue concebido y dado a luz durante la penosa travesía de la sierra, antes de la fundación de Macondo, y sus padres dieron gracias al cielo al comprobar que no tenía ningún órgano de animal. Aureliano, el primer ser humano que nació en Macondo, iba a cumplir seis años en marzo. Era silencioso y retraído. Había llorado en el vientre de su madre y nació con los ojos abiertos» (p. 20). Aureliano is small, intuitive, imaginative, and solitary, whereas José Arcadio is muscular, large, unimaginative, sexually active, noisy, and likes to carouse. The next pair of brothers, as Josefina Ludmer explains, continues this basic division: «Aureliano se opone a José Arcadio en el primer par como, en el segundo, Aureliano José a Arcadio (en realidad se llamó José Arcadio, pero le nombraban Arcadio para evitar confusiones.»[5] The oppositions continued by Pilar Ternera's offspring produce the following patterns: Aureliano—Pilar Ternera—Aureliano José and José Arcadio—Pilar Ternera—Arcadio. As Josefina Ludmer states: «En este par se repiten las oposiciones término por término. Arcadio tiene la fuerza brutal de su padre y se llama como él pero lleva a cabo funciones de Aureliano, su tío; pertenece a la esfera del lenguaje y de la acción política; Aureliano José, semejante físicamente a Aureliano y con su mismo nombre se ubica, en cuanto a sus funciones, en la esfera de su tío, José Arcadio: inclinación al incesto, vocación concupiscente, desidia, paz.»[6]

The third pair, José Arcadio Segundo and Aureliano Segundo, «hasta el principio de la adolescencia fueron dos mecanismos sincrónicos. Despertaban al mismo tiempo, sentían deseos de ir al baño a la misma hora, sufrían los mismos trastornos de salud y hasta soñaban las mismas cosas» (pp. 159-60). After adolescence, as Josefina Ludmer explains, «el que lleva desde entonces el nombre de José Arcadio Segundo (el 'supuesto' José Arcadio Segundo, porque en el cambio de nombres éste le tocó en definitiva, pero es un nombre incierto) es semejante al primer Aureliano: óseo, lineal y triste, pero desarrolla actividades propias del grupo que inauguró José Arcadio; lo mismo ocurre, en forma simétrica e inversa, con Aureliano Segundo: es monumental pero ensimismado; entra en el cuarto de Melquíades y habla con él.»[7] As the twins start to differ, they continue to play the game of mirrors, repeating and inverting oppositions from the previous generations until they merge again in death. In the last pair, José Arcadio Buendía and Aureliano Babilonia, the systems of oppositions cease, and all the characteristics of the Buendía men merge in Aureliano Babilonia who commits incest and deciphers the parchments. He is the only Buendía male whose father is an outsider (Mauricio Babilonia, the mechanic for the Banana company). Aureliano's activity remains strictly intellectual until Amaranta Ursula arrives, and he is the logical progression from the twins, since he condenses the Buendía's dual masculine line into one person. The final José Arcadio Buendía is no longer a Buendía, and he resembles his mother Fernanda.

The female side of the Buendías presents the same symmetries and contrasts as the males. The internal members are Ursula Iguarán, Amaranta, Remedios, la bella, Meme and Amaranta Ursula. The concubines are Pilar Ternera and Petra Cotes. Rebeca Remedios, Santa Sofía de la Piedad and Fernanda are married to Buendía men. Ursula is by far the most dominant figure, and she spans every generation except the last. She imposes order on the chaotic world of the Buendía men, and she is deeply rooted in daily reality. In the first chapter, she opposes every crazy project which her husband undertakes, and her physical capacities are almost inexhaustible: «La laboriosidad de Ursula andaba a la par con la de su marido. Activa, menuda, severa, aquella mujer de nervios inquebrantables, a quien en ningún momento de su vida se la oyó cantar, parecía estar en todas partes desde el amanecer hasta muy entrada la noche, siempre perseguida por el suave susurro de sus pollerines de olán. Gracias a ella, los pisos de tierra golpeada, los muros de barro sin encalar, los rústicos muebles de madera construidos por ellos mismos estaban siempre limpios, y los viejos arcones donde se guardaba la ropa exhalaban un tibio olor de albahaca» (p. 15). She undertakes several enlargements of the house in order to accommodate the increasing size of the family. Realizing that more room was needed, she «sacó el dinero acumulado en largos años de dura labor, adquirió compromisos de sus clientes, y emprendió la ampliación de la casa» (p. 53). The house symbolizes all of her characteristics: hospitality, vitality and a never-ending struggle to impose order on the disorganized males. If Ursula epitomizes common sense and order, she also possesses two other characteristics which she transmits to her descendants: the fear of marriage and incest. Amaranta inherits her fear of marriage and remains a virgin all her life. Amaranta and Rebeca differ in their respective attitudes towards love. When Pietro Crespi expresses his preference for Rebeca, Amaranta is filled with resentment towards her adopted sister. It remains with her until death and causes her to reject various suitors. Amaranta represses her sexual drives, whereas Rebeca suffers the pains of sexual desire. She returns to eating earth and sucking her thumb, and finally, José Arcadio rescues her with his volcanic virility. It is also in Chapter 4 that García Márquez develops the love story between Remedios and Aureliano. Remedios dies in childbirth, but she contrasts with both Aureliano and Rebeca. She attains an extraordinary maturity, despite her young age, and brings happiness to the Buendía household. She also resembles Ursula in her industriousness. Remedios, la bella, possesses the same innocence and beauty of the first Remedios, but her innocence reaches its purest form. Meme differs from all her female predecessors in that she incorporates a wider spectrum of family traits: «Pero al contrario de Amaranta, al contrario de todos, Meme no revelaba todavía el sino solitario de la familia, y parecía enteramente conforme con el mundo, aun cuando se encerraba en la sala a los dos de la tarde a practicar el clavicordio con una disciplina inflexible. Era evidente que le gustaba la casa, que pasaba todo el año soñando con el alboroto de adolescentes que provocaba su llegada, y que no andaba muy lejos de la vocación festiva y los desafueros hospitalarios de su padre. El primer signo de esa herencia calamitosa se reveló en las terceras vacaciones, cuando Meme apareció en la casa con cuatro monjas y sesenta y ocho compañeras de clase, a quienes invitó a pasar una semana en familia, por propia iniciativa y sin ningún anuncio» (p. 223). Meme is also the first Buendía woman to leave Macondo to study, and she participates in activities and relationships formerly reserved only for the men. She contrasts with Fernanda's closed mind and strictly limited world, and she breathes new life into the household: «Tenía un espíritu moderno que lastimaba la anticuada sobriedad y mal disimulado corazón cicatero de Fernanda, y que en cambio Aureliano Segundo se complacía en patrocinar» (p. 233). Meme, whom Fernanda finally cloisters in a monastery after her love affair with Mauricio Babilonia, resembles the Buendía men more than the women. Amaranta Ursula, like Aureliano, combines all the characteristics of the Buendía women: «Activa, menuda, indomable, como Ursula, y casi tan bella y provocativa como Remedios, la bella, estaba dotada de un raro instinto para anticiparse a la moda» (p. 319). In Amaranta Ursula, the feminine line reaches its final synthesis and conclusion.

The external women also fulfill various roles and functions in the Buendía clan. Santa Sofía de la Piedad, wife of Arcadio, acts in a manner which coincides perfectly with her name. She is unobtrusive, timid, and completely loyal to Ursula. She is so unassuming that when Fernanda arrives at the house, she «tuvo motivos para creer que era una sirvienta eternizada» (p. 303). Another contrast is seen between Ursula and Pilar Ternera. Pilar is the illegitimate cofounder of the Buendía clan, and her sexual prowess contrasts with Ursula's fear of it. Pilar Ternera also differs from Úrsula in her taste for magic and card reading. Like Ursula, her life and influence extend to all the generations of the Buendías whose hearts hide no secrets from her. Petra Cotes resembles Pilar Ternera in several ways. Her sexual appetite produces an incredible proliferation of animals, instead of children. Her gaiety and sensuality contrast with Fernanda's frigidity and narrowmindedness. Fernanda serves as a negative contrast to both Ursula and Petra Cotes directly, and indirectly to other women like her daughter Meme. Fernanda's negativity stands in direct opposition to Ursula who is open, hospitable and generous, whereas Fernanda is closed, fanatic, inhospitable and snobbish. Ursula immerses herself in daily life, whereas Fernanda lives in a kind of medieval past. Ursula accepts all members of the family, legitimate or not, but Fernanda refuses Meme's illegitimate child.

The structure of the Buendía family, in both its patriarchal and matriarchal lineages, involves a continuous process built upon parallels, contrasts, variations, and repetitions which appear in every generation. The two lineages describe a circle which closes itself in the end with the actual commission of incest. The patrilineal descent seems to form a more closed system than the matrilineal one. First of all, it involves only internal members who, after José Arcadio Buendía, form contraşting-similar pairs who exchange characteristics during their lifetimes: José Arcadio—Aureliano, Arcadio—Aureliano José, José Arcadio Segundo—Aureliano Segundo and José Arcadio—Aureliano. The intricate system of interchanging differences and similarities is broken in the last pairing when Aureliano (Babilonia) brings together all the Buendía male traits and terminates the line. In a sense, the patriarchal line follows the Hegelian dialectic: Thesis—José Arcadio Buendía; Antithesis—the successive pairings; and Synthesis—Aureliano (José Arcadio no longer belongs to the Buendía clan). In the thesis represented by José Arcadio Buendía is found a division between what Josefina Ludmer calls «cuerpo» and «mente.»[8] This opposition is then worked out in the antithesis by the three pairings. In the synthesis, the mind/body duality merges in Aureliano. As Josefina Ludmer states: «A lo largo del relato, hasta el fin del par de los gemelos, ambos órdenes han sido formalmente equivalentes. En el último par la negación de José Arcadio Buendía (su expulsión fuera del sistema, y la negación correlativa de la clase 'cuerpo,' con su decadencia y desvirilización), es decir la negación de uno de los términos de oposición.»[9] Aureliano, whose only activity is intellectual, takes over the body function when he meets Amaranta Ursula. Ludmer outlines the basic system of oppositions among the males in the following manner:

    1. Apertura de la ficción: José Arcadio Buendía (*unidad dual*)
    2. Escisión de la unidad en sus dos hijos: *oposición disyuntiva* de los dos primeros pares (Aureliano/José Arcadio, Arcadio/Aureliano José)
    3. Los gemelos, *oposición no disyuntiva,* dualidad ambivalente
    4. Cierre de la ficción: Aureliano Babilonia *(unidad dual)*

Las organizaciones 1 y 2 se encuentran en la primera inscripción; las 3 y 4 en la segunda; la figura 1 se relaciona estrechamente con el nacimiento de la ficción y sus condiciones de posibilidad; la 4 con el fin y el cierre del relato y las condiciones de su lectura.[10]

In Hegelian terminology, then, number one would correspond to the thesis, numbers 2 and 3 to the antithesis, and number 4 to the synthesis. The synthesis achieved in the male lineage is a circular one, and the apparently linear path of the Buendía's male line thus follows a circular path back to the initial duality in José Arcadio Buendía.

Partriarchy in *CAS* does not seem to conform to the strict idea of lineal progression that is normally attributed to it in Western culture. The father becomes the source of authority, continuation, and preservation, and all the other members must obey him. Vargas Llosa maintains that, in the Buendía family, a strict division guarantees the inferiority of the women, but a closer examination reveals some striking flaws in this patriarchal domination. The rise of patriarchy seems much more the result of social conditions than of some biological imperative. As Robert Briffault explains: «Some writers have supposed that the high status of women in certain communities is the outcome of special economic conditions, such as their having acquired land or property, and thus that this is a late development; but the fact that matriarchal organizations exist in societies which have the barest minimum of economic development, such as those of the Seri Indians, disposes of this explanation. Furthermore, there is no evidence of a transition from patriarchal to matriarchal customs anywhere. On the other hand, in every society, uncultured or not, where patriarchal usages obtain at the present day, indications are to be found of a previous higher status of women or of an actual matriarchal organization.»[11] José Arcadio Buendía hardly exercises his patriarchal duties in any traditional sense. He appears, at the outset, to be a typical patriarch, overseeing the organization and maintenance of Macondo, but this image soon vanishes under Melquíades' influence. When José Arcadio Buendía unleashes his imagination, he forgets his patriarchal duties, his sense of family disappears, and he absorbs himself in his experiments and imagination. Everything he does contradicts the logic and order associated with patriarchy. He makes no mention of his descendants when he and Ursula finally have sexual relations, and he dismisses her fear of incest by saying: «Si has de parir iguanas, criaremos iguanas» (p. 26) José Arcadio Buendía founds Macondo as a result of a dream, and he «no logró descifrar el sueño de las casas con paredes de espejos hasta el día en que conoció el hielo» (p. 28). The foundation of Macondo is not definitive, and, after his absurd expedition, he proposes to move Macondo to another site, but Ursula foils his plan. When Ursula advises him to take more interest in his children, he «miró a través de la ventana y vio a los dos niños descalzos en la huerta soleada, y tuvo la impresión de que sólo en aquel instante habían empezado a existir, concebidos por el conjuro de Ursula» (p. 20). This hardly characterizes the normal conception of the patriarch. In each generation, the Buendía men disobey the patriarchal imperative. Most notorious is Colonel Aureliano Buendía, whose activities obey no logic and lead absolutely nowhere. He not only scatters his semen all over the countryside, producing 17 illegitimate sons, but his only contribution to the Buendía lineage takes place by a union with Pilar Ternera, the illicit cofounder of the clan. Aureliano forsakes his family, his home, and his patriarchal duties and, instead, channels all of his energies into Petra Cotes. Their relationship produces an endless proliferation of animals, raffles, fiestas, and carnivals which convert patriarchy into purposeless play. The only activities in which the succeeding Buendía men participate with any regularity are the deciphering of Melquíades' manuscripts and alchemy. These activities have little to do with patriarchy, but they engage their excessive imaginations inherited from the founder.

The subversion of the patriarchal mandate also extends to the succession of generations. In the patriarchal family, each new addition should guarantee the orderly transition of authority from one generation to another. As each preceding generation ages, veneration and respect should be accorded to the older members. This is hardly the case with José Aradio Buendía. He spends the last part of his life tied to a tree and dies in the solitude of his own imagination. The Colonel, after being venerated and respected as a great general, is reduced to utter solitude and to making and remaking his little gold fish. If sexuality is the key to the continuation of the male line, then again it is converted in to a kind of purposeless activity which produces offsping almost by accident. For all the seismic, sexual power of the Buendía men, their adhesion to the principle of orderly succession is almost nonexistent. Aureliano and José Arcadio produce offspring from Pilar Ternera, not from their wives. Aureliano also produces 17 illegitimate offspring who, in turn, never reproduce. The intermingling of names also adds to the confusion, and the different generations of José Arcadios and Aurelianos engage in an intricate process of exchanging traits. The twins' similarities and differences so closely mirror each other that in death they become identical. The last pair graphically demonstrates the demise of the patriarchal imperative as José Arcadio is completely expelled from the Buendía clan. As one part dies, the other part is incorporated into Aureliano, whose final sexual act puts an end to the line. Every male member of the Buendía clan fails in one way or another to fit the pattern of patriarchy.

In the female line, the traditional functions attributed to matriarchy are not so well-defined. Vargas Llosa sees the structure of the Buendía clan as typical of underdeveloped countries in which women play a subordinate role. In *CAS,* the males have forsaken their patriarchal duties, and the women must compensate. Ursula's role in the founding of Macondo is as much matriarchal as patriarchal. Her work capacity is equal to her husband's. José Arcadio Buendía soon lost his social initiative and «de emprendedor y limpio, José Arcadio Buendía se convirtió en un hombre de aspecto holgazán, descuidado en el vestir, con una barba salvaje que Ursula lograba cuadrar a duras penas con un cuchillo de cocina» (p. 16). When he fails to find the route leading to civilization, Ursula discovers it when she goes in search of José Arcadio. Again and again Ursula assumes the functions of the patriarch as the men abandon their patriarchal duties. Pilar Ternera also crosses the boundary lines in the sense that most of the males seek her out as an initiator into sex and as an amorous confidante. If her role is not primarily masculine in this case, she still fulfills the sexual vacuum left by Ursula. Pilar Ternera exercises the same control over the men in sexual matters which Ursula does in daily life. Meme and Amaranta Ursula break out of their domestic confinement, leaving Macondo to participate in the masculine realm. Meme's apparently rigorous discipline conceals her predilection for festive occasions which makes her resemble her father, Aureliano. Amaranta Ursula, who synthesizes the Buendía women, also revives the patriarchal concern, seen in Ursula, to make the lineage last and prosper. The female lineage of the Buendía clan involves a much more diverse group of people than the males who closely mirror each other from generation to generation. In terms of opposing-similar pairs, there are Remedios-Remedios, la bella, Ursula-Fernanda, Ursula-Pilar Ternera, Fernanda-Petra Cotes, Amaranta-Remedios, Amaranta-Rebeca, Meme-Fernanda, Santa Sofía-Fernanda, etc. The different-similar pairs are more varied in the matriarchal lineage and encompass a greater variety of characteristics and possible combinations. The male line follows a more closed trajectory in its circular path leading back to the beginning, and the women exercise both matriarchal and patriarchal functions. Not only do they care, share, sew, sweep, show love, endure childbirth, show pity and pride, but they restore order, carry out their tasks in an orderly fashion, oppose the excessive imaginations of the males, and keep the family intact. Logic, order, tradition and a sense of family typify the women as much as do the other traditional matriarchal functions associated with the domestic scene. It is primarily, then, in the matriarchal lineage, that masculine and feminine roles blend. The theme of incest and the

Oedipus myth also alter the masculine and feminine lineages.

CAS parallels the Oedipus myth in many ways. José Arcadio Buendía killed his friend, Prudencio Aguilar, and then had sexual relations with his own wife, Ursula, who was his cousin. She had refused because a family legend had prophesied that the child born of endogamic parents would have a pig's tail. The son of this couple commits figurative incest when he marries an adoptive sister (José Arcadio and Rebeca). These episodes correspond to the curse placed on Laius for his illicit love affairs that warned that if he had a son, this son would be his assassin. The birth of Oedipus, as in CAS, involves both the guilt of the father and the attempt at filicide. Besides Ursula's attempted prohibition, Fernanda tries to dissuade Meme from committing social incest with Mauricio Babilonia. The son of this union, Aureliano, will commit the actual incest with Amaranta Ursula and the prophecy is fulfilled. When Oedipus is born, Laius sends him away and abandons him. This also occurs with Arcadio and the last Aureliano. Ursula simply resisted the adoption of Arcadio, but Fernanda actually thinks about killing the last Aureliano. When Oedipus flees Corinth for fear of endangering his adoptive parents, he returns to his place of origin. In CAS, several characters make similar trips: José Arcadio leaves with the gypsies and returns to marry Rebeca; Aureliano José returns ready to marry Amaranta, his adoptive mother, who is his aunt; José Arcadio returns from Rome to find the image of Amaranta, his grandmother, and Amaranta Ursula returns and commits incest. Oedipus kills Laius in a narrow passage, and in CAS, this aspect takes various forms: José Arcadio Buendía killing his friend and then having sexual relations with his cousin; José Arcadio, who loved Amaranta, is drowned by children, etc. In CAS, the Sphinx is seen in the character of Amaranta who castigates all those who seek to penetrate the secret of her sexuality. As for the riddle, the manuscripts fulfill this function. Just as Oedipus deciphers the secret of his origins, so too the Buendías seek to decipher the manuscripts which, once deciphered, destroy them and Macondo. In a number of variants of the myth, Oedipus also kills himself. The following diagram shows how the Oedipus myth is incorporated into CAS:[11]

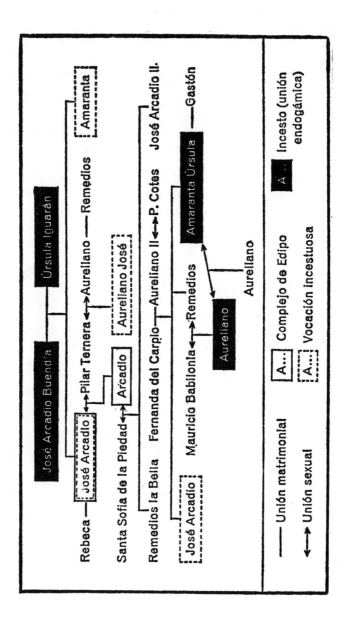

José Arcadio Buendía — Úrsula Iguarán

Rebeca — José Arcadio ⟷ Pilar Ternera ⟷ Aureliano — Remedios — Amaranta

Santa Sofía de la Piedad ⟷ Arcadio

Aureliano José

Remedios la Bella — Fernanda del Carpio — Aureliano II ⟷ P. Cotes — José Arcadio II.

Mauricio Babilonia ⟷ Remedios — Amaranta Úrsula — Gastón

José Arcadio — Aureliano

Aureliano

Leyenda:

—— Unión matrimonial

⟷ Unión sexual

A...	Complejo de Edipo
A...	Incesto (unión endogámica)
A...	Vocación incestuosa

García Márquez has applied a *bricolage* technique to the Oedipus myth in incorporating it into the novel. As Josefina Ludmer states: «Pero en *Cien años de soledad* no hay un solo hijo de alianzas culpables, un solo pariente adoptado, un solo personaje que intenta resolver el enigma, un solo viaje ni un solo crimen: el mito está significado a todo lo largo del relato por una pluralidad de elementos que son variados, escindidos, repetidos; en algunos personajes solo ocurre el viaje, en otros la adopción, en otros el crimen, en otros solo el desconocimiento de su identidad, en otros el deseo del incesto, y esta desconcentración es sintetizada en la última pareja de la ficción. A lo largo del relato solo actúan las unidades mínimas—los mitemas en la versión específica del relato—aisladas y no en el orden en que ocurren en la historia de Edipo: puede haber primero un incesto y luego un viaje; hay un gran hiperbatón narrativo; los personajes son simplemente el espacio donde esas unidades se permutan y desplazan; juegan, se combinan con otros.»[13] The Oedipus myth functions in the same way as the rest of the narrative units in the novel; that is, they obey the law of *bricolage* in which succession is more important than chronology. The myth becomes part of the telling process in which the storyteller uses *bricolage* to vary and order his finite elements without altering the basic message communicated by the myth. In *CAS,* the myth is varied, multiplied, and reordered to permeate the entire family structure, but it still remains the Oedipus myth.

Incest, an integral part of the Oedipus myth, manifests itself strongly in the Buendía clan. For García Márquez, incest does not possess the heavy stamp of degeneration and horror as in Faulkner. In *H,* the question of endogamic relationships is only alluded to by Isabel. In *FMG,* Big Mamá uses endogamy to insure the cohesion of her empire. In *CAS,* incest (real and imagined) runs through all the generations. As Lévi-Strauss says, «incest proper, and its metaphorical form as the violation of a minor (by someone 'old enough to be her father,' as the expression goes), even combines in some countries with its direct opposite, inter-racial sexual relations, an extreme form of exogamy, as the two most powerful inducements to horror and collective vengeance.»[14] The reaction to incest in *CAS* follows a double pattern of fear and attraction until it is finally committed at the end of the novel. Freud notes, in *Totem and Taboo,* the attraction of incest: «Psycho-analysis has taught us that a boy's earliest choice of objects for his love is incestuous and that those objects are forbidden ones—his mother and his sister. We have learnt, too, the manner in which, as he grows up, he liberates himself from this incestuous attraction. A neurotic, on the other hand, invariably exhibits some degree of physical infantilism. He has either failed to get free from the psycho-sexual conditions that prevailed in his childhood or he has returned to them—two possibilities which may be summed up as developmental inhibition and regression.»[15] That attraction and horror of incest are present in *CAS,* but García Márquez treats them quite differently. One could subject the different characters to close psychoanalytic scrutiny and produce a coherent analysis, but incest is much more important as a narrative element than as a part of the psychology of the characters. It is treated in the same *bricolage* fashion as the Oedipus myth, and is dispersed, multiplied, and inter-woven into the narrative fabric.

There are three aspects to incest in *CAS:* 1) The presence of an Oedipus complex in many characters; 2) the desire to commit incest in several characters; and 3) its actual commission by the first and last couples of the Buendía dynasty. The first category includes José Arcadio, Arcadio and Aureliano. When José Arcadio is with Pilar Ternera, «se encontraba con el rostro de Ursula, confusamente consciente de que estaba haciendo algo que desde hacía mucho tiempo deseaba que se pudiera hacer, pero que nunca se había imaginado que en realidad se pudiera hacer» (p. 31). José Arcadio and Aureliano regard Pilar Ternera more as a mother than a sex object. She fulfills the forbidden sexual attraction for the mother which Ursula cannot do, and she is the illicit cofounder of the Buendía clan. In the second category can be grouped Amaranta, José Arcadio, Aureliano José and José Arcadio. As Carmen Arnau says, «la vocación incestuosa es un rasgo característico de los Buendía, como ya se ha dicho; un cromosoma que pasa de generación en generación. Amaranta es la que siente más fuertemente esta atracción por el incesto, y cuando está a punto de realizarlo es siempre el temor del hijo con cola de cerdo lo que la retiene.»[16] In the third category, actual incest is carried out by José Arcadio Buendía and Ursula (endogamic relations) and by the last couple, Aureliano and Amaranta Ursula. Incest thus opens and closes the Buendía line, but what is surprising is that the horror and fear of incest are attenuated by the narrative. In the case of José Arcadio Buendía and Ursula, incest has a comic dimension. When he is confronted with the precedent of an uncle born with a pig's tail, his only response is: «No me importa tener cochinitos, siempre que puedan hablar» (p. 25). Instead of Ursula's fear of incest becoming serious, it is simply narrated with the same even tone as the other events. After killing Prudencio Augilar, José Arcadio Buendía settles the matter in one sentence. When Aureliano and Amaranta Ursula actually commit incest, no tragic pall hangs over it. The story of the

Buendía clan, with the Oedipus myth and incest as basic components, shows how myth deals narratively with the pure and impure on equal terms. Individual family members also play a significant role in the myth of Macondo, the most important of which are Ursula Iguarán, José Arcadio Buendía, Colonel Aureliano Buendía, and Melquíades.

Ursula Iguarán

The first image that comes to mind is that of the Great Mother who nourishes her race. There is the precedent of Big Mamá, who, despite being equipped to nourish her clan, dies a virgin. Ursula exhibits the same duality in that she is terrorized «con toda clase de pronósticos siniestros sobre su descendencia, hasta el extremo de conseguir que rehusara consumar el matrimonio» (p. 25). This fear remains with her, and Pilar Ternera fulfills the sexual function which Ursula cannot provide. Erich Neumann delineates two basic characters of the Feminine: «As *elementary character* we designate the aspect of the Feminine that as the Great Round, the Great Container, tends to hold fast to everything that springs from it and to surround it like an eternal substance. Everything born of it belongs to it and remains subject to it; and even if the individual becomes independent, the Archetypal Feminine relativizes this independence into a nonessential variant of her own perpetual being. The *transformative character* of the Feminine is the expression of a different fundamental psychic constellation, which is also connected with feminine symbolism. In the transformative character, the accent is on the dynamic element of the psyche, which, in contrast to the conservative tendency of the elementary character, drives toward motion, change, and in a word, transformation.»[17] Ursula combines both these characteristics in *CAS*. She demonstrates an overpowering effort to encompass all the members of her clan, and she also is extremely active in keeping the family intact. As Neumann says: «In other words, the two characters are not antithetical from the very start but interpenetrate and combine with one another in many ways, and it is only in unusual and extreme constellations that we find one or the other character isolated.»[18] Ursula does not confine her activities to the matriarchal realm. The men, in fact, abandon their patriarchal duties, and she fulfills them in their absence. It is obvious, in terms of the elementary charcter which typifies the matriarchal domain, that Ursula fulfills it in its broadest possible terms. Ursula's primary domain is the house, which mystics have traditionally considered as the feminine aspect of the universe. Ursula undertakes every enlargement of the house to encompass the growing clan, and she welcomes equally any legitimate or illegitimate member of the clan. Ricardo Gullón offers the following analysis: «El personaje eje es Ursula Iguarán, la mujer de José Arcadio Buendía (con quien forma la pareja inicial), la Madre, con mayúscula y minúscula; está presente en la mayor parte de la novela, formula algunas de las observaciones-clave, y además crea, por su actividad incesante, constructiva y 'normal,' doméstica, el centro en que acontecen episodios decisivos y otros germinan y se preparan.»[19] Ursula provides the boundaries of the daily world which allow the insertion of the marvelous. As is characteristic of the *bricolage* technique in *CAS,* the archetypal feminine is shared by Ursula and Pilar Ternera, and later, when Ursula's influence diminishes, by Fernanda and Petra Cotes in a reduced form. Ursula transfers the sexual function to Pilar Ternera in whom the Buendía men see a mother more than a sex object. Fernanda represents a negative portrait of the archetypal feminine, for she is diametrically opposed to Ursula in every way. Petra Cotes also represents a negative portrait of the sexual function in that she produces an endless number of animals, but no descendants. She does, however, fulfill Ursula's function by supporting the Buendía household after the great deluge. Ursula's sharing of the matriarchal domain with Pilar Ternera parallels the transformation of the pagan Earth Mother into the Virgin Mary: «La significación simbólica de María excede pues el esquema de María Virgen para enlazarse con la imagen de la Madre, vigente en las religiones arcaicas y conservada en ciertos cultos marianos, a la que encarna Pilar Ternera.»[20] Pilar Ternera represents, then, the initiator of the Buendía men into sexuality. As for Petra Cotes, she embodies the exaltation of fertility as practiced in archaic religions. Remedios (her young age and innocence) and Remedios, la bella, (pure innocence) form the counterparts of the Virgin Mary. These four women establish the link between the earth-mother, the primordial mother, and her reincarnation in more purified form in the Virgin Mary. As Amaury de Riencourt states: «Mary's virginity and the theme of the virgin birth were restatements of the old theme of the Great Mother Without a Spouse, a symbolic reformulation of the Paleolithic concept of woman being fertilized by a spiritual entity without need of male assistance, *conceptio immaculata.* In Mary, the Mother of God, what was left of the Magna Mater found a lasting reincarnation; in her tragedy the previous mythical *mater dolorosa,* Cybele, Isis and the others, could witness the reenactment of their own mythical tragedies. But, here again, her tragedy had really taken place in history, in the clear light of day; it was a historical fact, not merely a mythological dreamlike vision.»[21]

The archetypal value of Ursula is dispersed and multiplied in *CAS* until it pervades the different generations of Buendías. Everything is concentrated in Ursula in a way, for she is the initiator of the clan. In spite of her fear of sex, she does give birth to two sons who continue the lineage. Ursula's predominant image is her telluric, practical function and, as she ages, her matriarchal functions take precedence over all others. The sexual, fertility, and virginal aspects of the Archetypal Feminine are transferred to other women and then synthesized in Amaranta Ursula: «Por su parte Amaranta Ursula reúne ya definitivamente la imagen virginal de Amaranta, la erótica y primordial de Pilar Ternera y la telúrica y práctica de Ursula.»[22] Just as the Oedipus myth is reordered without changing its basic components, so too Ursula is multiplied, varied and reincarnated in different characters without changing her basic composition.

José Arcadio Buendía

José Arcadio Buendía is the patriarch of the Buendía clan who exercises his duties to a certain extent. On the one hand, he was a «patriarca juvenil» who was «el hombre más emprendedor que se veía jamás en la aldea» (p. 15). He devoted his enormous energies to developing Macondo into «una aldea más ordenada y laboriosa que cualquiera de las conocidas hasta entonces por sus 300 habitantes» (p. 16). His other side consists of an extravagant imagination which always exceeded the bounds of nature and undermined his social initiative. Graciela Maturo says that García Márquez wants to «presentar en José Arcadio Buendía un arquetipo humano: el varón justo y sabio que reparte el agua y la tierra entre los miembros de su tribu, el fundador de una ciudad—de un espacio sagrado—y de una familia que lo prolonga en la sangre y en el espíritu. Los lectores de *Cien años de soledad* han reconocido en él, por estas características, a Adán.»[23] José Arcadio Buendía's name (Arcadio = Arcadia and Buendía = dawning of the world) suggests the figure of the natural man. His reactions are more instinctual than intellectual when it comes to founding his clan. He also resembles Abraham in Genesis with the successive marriages based on a double lineage of wife (Ursula) and concubine (Pilar Ternera). Graciela Maturo also sees him as «el héroe civilizador, el iniciado, el patriarca que lleva al pueblo a la Tierra Prometida; pero es también el iniciado de los Nuevos Tiempos, el que muere atado al Arbol que pasa así a ser un equivalente simbólico de la Cruz.»[24] She also adds that «muchos son los símbolos e indicios que acompañan la figura de José Arcadio Buendía para señalarlo como Cristo, en una doble referencia histórica y mítica: los gallos de pelea; la lanza que blande para exterminar a Prudencio Aguilar.»[25]

The character of José Arcadio Buendía is complicated by the fact that he does not carry out the patriarchal functions, and Ursula must assume them. His actions are carried out in a *bricolage* way which negates patriarchy. His descendants, who exhibit the duality of mind/body, also repeat the *bricolage* actions of the father. The purposelessness of their activities opposes the notions of order and linear progression. The first chapter is a compendium of *bricolage* activities which serves as a paradigm of all the male members' actions. The dignity and order of the patriarch vanishes as José Arcadio Buendía hurtles himself into every activity which his imagination can invent to oppose orderliness. The sexual activity of the Buendía men is productive, but purposeless, and the succession of the generations is subject to chance. José Arcadio Buendía may well constitute an archetype of the founder, the patriarch, and Christ, but he is also a *bricoleur* par excellence. He is best described as an external-internal mytical figure. From an external point of view, he possesses certain charcteristics which link him to archetypal figures, and also repeats certain actions (the founding of a city and of a lineage, his link with Christ by being tied to a tree, his explorations, etc.) which constitute exemplary acts. In an internal sense, José Arcadio Buendía is also a character in novel, and his actions imitate the *bricolage* narration. Since the narrator is on equal terms with the characters, what he narrates unites him with the characters. He eliminates the divisions between matriarchal and patriarchal so that characters can perform both functions. This *bricolage* approach gives the mythical elements more flexibility because they can be applied to more characters. José Arcadio Buendía is the patriarch, but he also performs other functions not normally attributed to his role. The *what* and *how* of the narrative merge, and the reader can combine the external and internal mythical features of each character.

Colonel Aureliano Buendía

Colonel Aureliano Buendía follows the same internal and external pattern of his father. As Graciela Maturo says: «Todos los personajes que pertenecen al 'clan Buendía' se dibujan de un modo u otro sobre el arquetipo del fundador, al que he adjudicado los valores de Abraham y Cristo (Antigua y Nueva Alianza del pueblo elegido con Dios).»[26] She also adds that the Colonel's making of little gold fish establishes a double link with the founder: «El pez como símbolo de Cristo; el oro, de la vida espiritual que se contraponen con toda evidencia a los animalitos de caramelo que comercia Ursula. Aureliano parece hallar en esos trabajos un estímulo para su obstinación en la fidelidad a ciertos valores: la sacralidad, el sentimiento del honor, la vitalidad de la naturaleza, el respeto a los muertos. Lo que importa, se dice una y otra vez, es el *trabajo* y no un resultado ulterior.»[27] Aureliano, by his sexual relations with Pilar Ternera, also continues the Buendía lineage through a concubine. His primary importance, however, lies in his relationship to war and as an archetypal figure of the *caudillo* who was such a pervasive figure in Latin America's post-independence era. Colonel Aureliano Buendía is the most ubiquitous figure in García Márquez' fiction. He appears in *H, FMG,* and *El coronel no tiene quien le escriba,* and he dominates a good portion of *CAS.* Like many of the generals and *caudillos* who fought innumerable battles in nameless places, the Colonel is a prototype of these legendary figures. After Latin America gained independence in 1830, these *caudillos* filled the political vacuum left by Spain. García Márquez uses the process of depersonalization to portray and universalize Colonel Aureliano Buendía. Aureliano follows his father's evolution as a character by alternating periods of isolation and social participation. As Josefina Ludmer says: «La primera parte de Aureliano (encierro, castidad, trabajo artesanal, enamoramiento, poemas, matrimonio) se opone a la segunda (acción política, guerra, engendró muchos hijos) y ésta a la última: retorno al encierro y la castidad, fabricación circular de los pescados de oro.»[28] In the war phase, the Colonel is never seen in battle. The war, in fact, is simply described except for brief moments of concrete violence. He is seen in various locations which give both him and the war a great deal of spatio-temporal expansion: «Así empezó la leyenda de la ubicuidad del coronel Aureliano Buendía. Informaciones simultáneas y contradictorias lo declaraban victorioso en Villanueva, derrotado en Guacamayal, devorado por los indios Motilones, muerto en una aldea de la ciénaga y otra vez sublevado en Urumita» (p. 116). García Márquez depersonalizes the war so that it becomes a paradigm of all wars. He gives a condensed history of Colonel Aureliano Buendía's career on page 94, and then proceeds to expand both the Colonel and the war in time and space. Colonel Aureliano Buendía becomes commander of the liberal forces which oppose the conservative party. The liberal/conservative dichotomy is typical of the political divisions in the post-independence period, and many bloody wars were fought in the name of completely opposed ideologies.

His transformation recalls the way in which many military men quickly came to power. After overpowering the local militia in Macondo, «esa misma noche, mientras se escuchaban las descargas del pelotón de fusilamiento, Arcadio fue nombrado jefe civil y militar de la plaza» (p. 93). When Aureliano takes command, don Apolinar Moscote «tuvo dificultades para identificar aquel conspirador de botas altas y fusil terciado a la espalda con quien había jugado dominó hasta las nueve de la noche» (p. 93). When don Apolinar Moscote calls him Aurelito, he replies: «'Es la guerra. Y no me vuelva a decir Aurelito, que ya soy el coronel Aureliano Buendía'» (p. 93). Like many *caudillos,* his rise to power is meteoric. In *CAS* where characters exchange roles, José Arcadio becomes the image of the petty dictator: «Arcadio le dio una interpretación muy personal a la recomendación. Se inventó un uniforme con galones y charreteras de mariscal, inspirado en las láminas de un libro de Melquíades y se colgó al cinto el sable con borlas doradas del capitán fusilado» (p. 94). He quickly converts himself into «el más cruel de los gobernantes que hubo nunca en Macondo» (p. 95). Aureliano, in his childhood, was silent, reclusive, and engaged in solitary work, whereas José Arcadio was noisy, expansive, traveled a lot, and did not work. Now in their respective roles in the military, the opposition between them continues. Aureliano remains a solitary figure, but he becomes expansive by commanding the liberal forces. His name has a historic dimension, whereas José Arcadio is much more restricted. Arcadio's position as military and civil commander confirms his role of petty dictator and coincides with his reduction to a limited circle of attention. Aureliano's role as an archetypal figure of the *caudillo* and charismatic leader is marked by solitude and power which eventually escapes him: «Extraviado en la soledad de su inmenso poder, empezó a perder el rumbo. Le molestaba la gente que lo aclamaba en los pueblos vencidos, y que le parecía la misma que aclamaba al enemigo. Por todos partes encontraba adolescentes que lo miraban con sus propios ojos, que hablaban con su propia voz, que lo saludaban con la misma desconfianza con que él los saludaba a ellos y que decían ser sus hijos. Se sintió disperso, repetido y más solitario que nunca. Tuvo la convicción de que sus propios oficiales le mentían» (p. 146). The Colonel loses contact with reality, and exceeds its boundaries by inflating his ego. His orders «se cumplían antes de ser impartidas, aun antes de que él las concibiera, y siempre llegaban mucho más lejos de donde él se hubiera atrevido a hacerlas llegar» (p. 146). His most persistent memory concerns his discovery of ice, and it serves as a symbol for this man who is immersed in his own solitude. He encloses himself in a chalk circle which no one can enter. Finally, «huyendo del frío que había de acompañarlo hasta la muerte, buscó un último refugio en Macondo, al calor de sus recuerdos más antiguos» (p. 147). Ice is closely associated with cold, which «corresponds symbolically to being in the situation of, or longing for, solitude or exaltation.»[29] The Colonel seeks solitude, even though he engages in the political and public life of the country. It becomes an expansive solitude which then contracts when he returns to Macondo where he limits himself to making little gold fish in an endless cycle. Julio Ortega says that «sobre aquel tiempo mítico las guerras del coronel Aureliano Buendía señalan que Macondo ha entrado a formar parte de un tiempo más concreto, insertado ya a una situación histórica. Así, el tiempo se hace histórico.»[30] The Colonel violates this historical time by trying to destroy everything that it creates through his absurd wars. As Julio Ortega declares, these chaotic activities «sugieren en la novela la locura que amenaza a esta historia, su íntima confusión y su impulso destructor. La misma sed de justicia termina convirtiéndose en una matanza ciega.»[31] The Colonel is expelled from the mythical world of Macondo and condemned to a state of isolation and solitude. He can neither recall his dreams, nor can he see his dead father, nor talk with Melquíades. When he dies, no supernatural manifestations accompany his death. As Ariel Dorfman says: «La exageración de su *ego*, su orgullo desmesurado, que desea expandirse hasta aplastar todo vestigio de lo que no refleja su punto de vista, termina por convertirlo en una nada que ni siquiera controla sus propios pensamientos, en intermediario entre la realidad que se mueve en cierta dirección y sus pensamientos que deciden con retraso el mismo curso.»[32] The Colonel is always flirting with death, but his own is nothing but a banal imitation of the magic and fantastic deaths of the other characters. The Colonel is also a destructive version of the *bricoleur,* because, instead of creating something new, he destroys the finite elements with which he is working. The chaos of war corresponds to the Colonel's unbridled, chaotic manner of acting. José Arcadio Buendía acted in much the same way, but mythical time allowed for his excesses. The Colonel's actions take place in a linear world in which actions are supposed to follow a causal order. His excesses can no longer be harmless, and the result is utter chaos and destruction. *Bricolage* actions are not suited to linear time, and the result is utter confusion. The move into history causes Aureliano to be expelled from mythical time and place, and his return to Macondo does not allow him to reincorporate himself into the family. He has lost his mythical identity.

Melquíades

Melquíades represents many different aspects in the novel, like the mysterious priest of Salem in the *Bible,* called Melchizedek, who blessed Abraham in the name of God, and also represented a type of Christ, the Priest King. Melquíades is also the master alchemist, and introduces the Buendía men into the realm of the fantastic. He is a ubiquitous figure, appearing and disappearing at different intervals. He may also be a persona of the narrator, for he has written the Buendía history in Sanskrit. Despite all his magical, mysterious powers, «tenía un peso humano, una condición terrestre que lo mantenía enredado en los minúsculos problemas de la vida cotidiana. Se quejaba de dolencias de viejo, sufría por los más insignificantes percances económicos y había dejado de reír desde hacía mucho tiempo, porque el escorbuto le había arrancado los dientes» (p. 13). He creates the magical, marvelous space in the novel, just as Ursula produces the space of daily reality. In the first chapter, with the successive returns of the gypsies, José Arcadio Buendía's enthusiasm for all the crazy inventions, and Ursula's constant opposition, the two spaces collide, then finally merge at the end of the chapter. The gypsies bring the secret of the ages including «el conocimiento hermético a cuya vasta familia pertenece la alquimia.»[33] Melquíades' alchemy links him most closely to myth.

Near the end of *CAS* it is revealed that Melquíades had written the story of the family «hasta en sus detalles más triviales con cien años de anticipación» (p. 349). Like coded, alchemical books, he had written it «en sánscrito, que era su lengua materna, y había cifrado los versos pares con la clave privada del emperador Augusto y los impares con claves militares lacedemonias» (p. 349). Sanskrit represents a kind of *superlangue,* or coded message, in Lévi-Strauss' definition of myth. Melquíades orders events of the story in a *bricolage* manner: «La protección final radicaba en que Melquíades no había ordenado los hechos en el tiempo convencional de los hombres, sino que concentró un siglo de episodios cotidianos, de modo que todos coexistieran en un instante» (pp. 349-50). Since all the events have equal value, they are not ordered according to chronology. Alchemy, too, is a *bricolage* science which pervades the whole novel. After his death, Melquíades returns in order to communicate with the different Buendía men, and his room remains impervious to the effects of time. The alchemists tried to combine opposites to produce unity, and many times they proceeded in a *bricolage* fashion to accomplish their task. Their seemingly illogical combinations represented a rival creation to the orderly universe. Melquíades is the primary representative of the *bricolage* universe that he opens up to the Buendía men, and alchemy provides him with the necessary tools. Mythical, circular time characterizes the *bricolage* universe, and the Buendía men undertake their activities within this framework. Since they do not have to progress in a linear fashion, their projects either end at the beginning, or they never accomplish what they set out to do. Melquíades opposes the orderly, linear universe of Western man, and he turns the Buendía men into *bricoleurs* who join him in his subversive act. Every facet of *CAS*'s mythical characters can be placed under the sign of *bricolage* which makes room for all the competing elements. As Patricia Tobin says: «By extension, Ursula's maternal care may be seen in its generalized aspect as the diffusive accommodation of 'everything' by the narrative: like Ursula, the novel extends welcome to a richly abundant reality, regardless of its potential for dissonance and exclusion, and holds all chaos within community.»[34]

NOTES

1. Josefina Ludmer, *Cien años de soledad: una interpretación* (Buenos Aires: Editorial Tiempo Contemporáneo, 1972), p. 9.

2. Mario Vargas Llosa, *García Márquez: historia de un deicidio* (Barcelona: Barral Editores, 1971), pp. 503-4.

3. *Ibid.*, p. 504.

4. *Ibid.*, p. 504.

5. Ludmer, p. 65.

6. *Ibid,* p. 69.

7. *Ibid.,* p. 160.

8. *Ibid.,* p. 191.

9. *Ibid.,* p. 188.

10. *Ibid.,* p. 169.

11. Robert Briffault, *The Mothers* (New York: The Macmillan Company, 1959), p. 73.

12. Carmen Arnau, *El mundo mítico de Gabriel García Márquez* (Barcelona: Ediciones Península, 1971), p. 86.

13. Ludmer, pp. 27-8.

14. Claude Lévi-Strauss, *The Elementary Structures of Kinship,* trans. James Harle Bell, John Richard von Sturmer and Rodney Needham (Boston: Beacon Press, 1969), p. 10.

15. Sigmund Freud, *Totem and Taboo,* trans. James Strachey (New York: W. W. Norton and Company, Inc., 1950). p. 17.

16. Arnau, pp. 90-1.

17. Erich Neumann, *The Great Mother,* trans. Ralph Manheim (Princeton: Princeton University Press, 1963), pp. 25, 28-9.

18. *Ibid.,* p. 29.

19. Ricardo Gullón, *García Márquez o el olvidado arte de contar* (Madrid: Taurus Ediciones, 1970), p. 25.

20. Graciela Maturo, *Claves simbólicas de Gabriel García Márquez* (Buenos Aires: Fernando García Cambeiro, 1972), p. 145.

21. Amaury de Riencourt, *Sex and Power in History* (New York: Dell Publishing Co., Inc., 1974), p. 144.

22. Maturo, p. 148.

23. *Ibid.,* pp. 117-18.

24. *Ibid.,* p. 119.

25. *Ibid.,* p. 119.

26. *ibid.,* pp. 122-3.

27. *Ibid.,* pp. 123.

28. Ludmer, p. 63.

29. J. E. Cirlot, *A Dictionary of Symbols,* trans. Jack Sage (New York: Philosophical Library, Inc., 1963), p. 49.

30. Julio Ortega, *La contemplación y la fiesta* (Caracas: Monte Avila Editores, C. A., 1969), p. 121.

31. *Ibid.,* p. 122.

32. Ariel Dorfman, «La muerte como acto imaginativo en *Cien años de soledad,*» in *Homenaje a Gabriel García Márquez,* ed. Helmy F. Giacoman (New York: Las Américas Publishing Company, Inc., 1972), p. 118.

33. Maturo, p. 127.

34. Patricia Drechsel Tobin, *Time and the Novel: The Genealogical Imperative* (Princeton: Princeton University Press, 1978), p. 187.

HISTORY, MYTH AND TIME IN MACONDO

CHAPTER 7

Most of García Márquez' fiction is situated in Macondo, but some of his other works are located in «el pueblo.» He has stated that «ni *El coronel no tiene quien le escriba* ni *La mala hora,* ni la mayoría de los cuentos de *Los funerales de la Mamá Grande* ocurren en Macondo. Ocurren en Macondo *La hojarasca* y *Cien años de soledad.*»[1] The problem is complicated by the fact that his previous works contain allusions and elements which appear in *CAS.* Colonel Aureliano Buendía is referred to in *H, El coronel no tiene quien le escriba* and *FMG.* The almond trees planted by Macondo's founder, José Arcadio Buendía, appear in both Macondo and «el pueblo.» Macondo and «el pueblo» share other similarities. Their climates exhibit alternating periods of intense, unbearable heat and heavy rain. Violence, both personal and political, erupts in both towns. As Olga Carreras González says: «El alcalde de *La hojarasca* y el de *La mala hora* tienen muchos aspectos en común, al igual que los coroneles de sus obras. Presagios, señales de mal agüero y presentimientos aparecen en casi todas, así la Casandra de *La mala hora* anticipa el personaje de Pilar Ternera en *Cien años de soledad.* La pasión sexual desorbitada de los Buendía se preanuncia en los excesos eróticos del juez Arcadio en *La mala hora.* La soledad del déspota que se ejemplifica magistralmente en el coronel Aureliano Buendía, se anticipa en los rasgos de la vida del alcalde mostrados en *La mala hora*».[2] One way to resolve the problem is to see where these works fall in García Márquez' evolution.

García Márquez followed two different paths before arriving at *CAS:* one political and the other mythical. *H,* the short story «Los funerales de la Mamá Grande» and *CAS* belong to the mythical, and *El coronel no tiene quien le escriba* and *La mala hora* to the political. Both paths lead to *CAS* in which García Márquez adds, deletes, modifies and incorporates material from both «el pueblo» and Macondo. Three other short stories, «La siesta del martes,» «Un día después del sábado» and «Isabel viendo llover en Macondo» also take place in Macondo. In general, the more realistic novels take place in «el pueblo» and the more magical ones unfold in Macondo. This dual evolution can be outlined in the following manner:

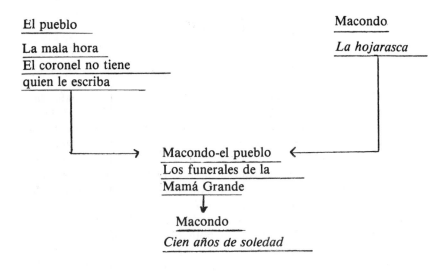

Macondo absorbs «el pueblo» in *CAS* and certainly overshadows it in his earlier fiction. In a general way, Macondo is the only setting for his fiction because «los rasgos de Macondo se muestran a lo largo de toda ella, aunque sólo alcancen su clímax y consagración en dicha novela. Ese pueblo innominado en el que el autor trata de situar algunos de sus cuentos y novelas no es sino el mismo Macondo, menos fantasmal quizás, más cotidiano y real, pero Macondo con su calor infernal, con su olor a podredumbre y con la carga insoportable de su soledad.»[3]

The most complete perspective of Macondo before *CAS* is found in *H*. Macondo is in a moribund state, decaying slowly from within. As Isabel says: «Es como si Dios hubiera declarado innecesario a Macondo y lo hubiera echado al rincón donde están los pueblos que han dejado de prestar servicio a la creación» (p. 127). This same vision of Macondo also appears in the short story entitled «Isabel viendo llover en Macondo.» The rain paralyzes Macondo and renders it helpless: «Estábamos paralizados, narcotizados por la lluvia, entregados al derrumbamiento de la naturaleza en una actitud pacífica y resignada.»' Nature assaults Macondo and detaches it from time. Isabel exclaims at the end: «'Dios mío'—pensé entonces, confundida por el trastorno del tiempo. 'Ahora no me sorprendería de que me llamaran para asistir a la misa del domingo pasado'» (p. 20). The cycles of heat and rain affect Macondo much as they would a person sensitive to the elements. In *H,* the idea of progress clashes with Macondo's internal time. The Colonel says in the prologue that «la hojarasca era implacable. Todo lo contaminaba de su revuelto olor multitudinario, olor de secreción a flor de piel y de recóndita muerte. En menos de un año arrojó sobre el pueblo los escombros de numerosas catástrofes anteriores a ella misma, esparció en las calles su confusa carga de desperdicios» (p. 9). Macondo became «un pueblo diferente y complicado, hecho con los desperdicios de los otros pueblos» (p. 9). Progress is not welcome, for it disrupts the tradition-bound evolution and hierarchy in Macondo. Progress brings with it another unwelcome guest, linear time, which is particularly devastating for Macondo. Linear time is very strong in *H,* and the three narrators measure Macondo's rise and fall in chronological terms. The Colonel says: «Para entonces, la compañía bananera había acabado de exprimirnos, y se había ido de Macondo con los desperdicios de los desperdicios que nos había traído. Y con ellos se había ido la hojarasca, los últimos rastros de lo que fue el próspero Macondo» (p. 110). Mythical timelessness appears in the form of circular time which is associated with the period of Macondo's decay. The Colonel and Isabel reveal it in their monologues, but linear time has disrupted Macondo's internal equilibrium. Macondo's history in *H* is a shortened version of what will appear in *CAS,* but many events are only foreshadowed; that is, the effects of these events are given without the causes. These adumbrated events include Macondo's founding, the banana company, the arrival of progress, Macondo's economic apogee, the civil war, the journey across the mountains, and the references to Colonel Aureliano Buendía.

In *FMG,* a different Macondo emerges. It is no longer a question of presenting a microhistory of the town, and the only unexplained allusion is to the civil war. Macondo is under the matriarchal rule of Big Mamá, and there are no dates to mark out Macondo's history. The only date, 1875, places Macondo in some historical period after the war. What is significant is Macondo's geographical situation, and it is seen both in microcosmic and macrocosmic terms. The reader learns that «en realidad, esa era la única cosecha que jamás recogió la familia de un territorio muerto desde sus orígenes, calculado a primera vista en 100.000 hectáreas. Pero las circunstancias históricas habían dispuesto que dentro de esos límites crecieran y prosperaran las seis poblaciones del distrito de Macondo, incluso la cabecera del municipio» (p. 135). When Big Mamá is buried, people from many different places attend her funeral like la Guajira, el Sinú, Guacamayal, la Sierpe, Aracataca, the capital, and even Rome. Time and space contract and protract in order to accommodate all the elements associated with Macondo, and its evolution is no longer governed by linear time. Macondo can be simultaneously a «distrito de calor y malaria, cuyo nombre se ignoraba en el resto del país» (p. 138) and the *axis mundi* of all the fantastic and mythical events associated with it. In *FMG*, Macondo undergoes a process of mythical expansion which allows it to encompass everything in its realm. The specific and the universal occupy the same space and time, and Macondo moves toward the mythical timelessness of *CAS*.

In *CAS*, specific information is provided about Macondo's location which corresponds to Aracataca, Colombia, in the Department of the Magdalena where García Márquez was born in 1928: «José Arcadio Buendía ignoraba por completo la geografía de la región. Sabía que hacia el oriente estaba la sierra impenetrable, y al otro lado de la sierra la antigua ciudad de Riohacha...Al sur estaban los pantanos, cubiertos de una eterna nata vegetal, y el vasto universo de la ciénaga grande, que según testimonio de los gitanos carecía de límites. La ciénaga grande se confundía al occidente con una extensión acuática sin horizontes» (pp. 16-17). If this description is compared to a map of the Department of the Magdalena, it can be seen that the Sierra Nevada de Santa Marta lies to the east of Aracataca, and Riohacha is located on the other side of the mountains. A swampy region lies to the south of Aracataca. To the west extend an aquatic area (Ciénaga Grande Santa Marta) and the Atlantic Ocean that, in *CAS*, become the «extensión acuática sin horizontes.» José Arcadio Buendía wanted to establish contact with civilization and followed the route to the north. He and his men ended their expedition at the edge of the sea which is the Atlantic Ocean on the map.

Although Macondo's history does not follow any definite chronology, its principal stages can nevertheless be established:

1. Discovery and founding of Macondo (pp. 9-29)
2. Patriarchal regime (pp. 30-54)
3. Installation of civil and religious authorities (pp. 54-87)
4. The civil war (pp. 88-154)

5. Progress and the family situation (pp. 155-195)
6. The period of the banana fever (pp. 195-266)
7. Decadence and final destruction of Macondo and the Buendía family (pp. 266-351)

The discovery and founding of Macondo parallel Spain's discovery, conquest and settlement of Latin America. After killing Prudencio Aguilar in a fight, José Arcadio Buendía, his wife, Ursula Iguarán, and a group of followers set out to establish a new town. The discovery and exploration preceding Macondo's foundation are evoked by the objects that Spanish explorers used. During José Arcadio Buendía's exploration of the region surrounding Macondo, he unearthed «una armadura del siglo XV con todas sus partes soldadas por un cascote de óxido» (p. 10). When he failed to find a route linking Macondo to the outside world, he found only the charred hull of a Spanish galleon: «Frente a ellos, rodeado de helechos y palmeras, blanco y polvoriento en la silenciosa luz de la mañana, estaba un enorme galeón español» (p. 18). Other references to the tools of exploration also suggest this period: «De su puño y letra escribió /Melquíades/ una apretada síntesis de los estudios del monje Hermann, que dejó a su disposición para que /José Arcadio Buendía/ pudiera servisrse del astrolabio, la brújula y el sextante» (p. 11). The newness of Latin America is presented in the opening page: «El mundo era tan reciente, que muchas cosas carecían de nombre, y para mencionarlas había que señalarlas con el dedo» (p. 9). Spanish explorers also had to invent new names for the objects they found. José Arcadio Buendía's expedition resembles those of the Spanish explorers who ventured into uncharted territory: «No se trazaron un itinerario definido. Solamente procuraban viajar en sentido contrario al camino de Riohacha para no dejar ningún rastro ni encontrar gente conocida. Fue un viaje absurdo» (p. 27). The Spanish explorers also founded towns in the much the same way as José Arcadio Buendía: «Al día siguiente convenció a sus hombres de que nunca encontrarían el mar. Les ordenó derribar los árboles para hacer un claro junto al río, en el lugar más fresco de la orilla, y allí fundaron la aldea» (p. 28) José Arcadio Buendía, like many explorers, made an astounding discovery: «La tierra es redonda como una naranja» (p. 12). Other historical references are also made to the English pirate Sir Francis Drake: «...según le había contado el primer Aureliano Buendía, su abuelo—Sir Francis Drake se daba al deporte de cazar caimanes a cañonazos, que luego hacía remendar y rellenar de paja para llevárselos a la reina Isabel» (p. 16); and: «Cuando el pirata Francis

Drake asaltó a Riohacha, en el siglo XVI, la bisabuela de Ursula Iguarán se asustó tanto con el toque de rebato y el estampido de los cañones, que perdió el control de los nervios y se sentó en un fogón encendido» (p 24). England, France and Holland undertook a campaign of piracy against Spain in order to break its trade monopoly, and Sir Francis Drake carried out much of the plundering of Spanish ships during Elizabeth I's reign.

The Buendías govern Macondo in a benevolent, fluid way which recalls Rousseau's state of nature in his *Social Contract*. The artificial barriers between men have not yet been solidified, and Macondo exists in a historical vacuum in which time seems suspended: «Era en verdad una aldea feliz, donde nadie era mayor de treinta años y donde nadie había muerto» (p. 16); «Como en aquel tiempo no había cementerio en Macondo, pues hasta entonces no había muerto nadie» (pp. 42-3). Soon, however, reality invades Macondo, and its timeless existence abruptly ends with the installation of civil and religious authorities. The arrival of don Apolinar Moscote marks the beginning of civil authority: «Don Apolinar Moscote, el corregidor, había llegado a Macondo sin hacer ruido. Puso una mesa y una silla que les compró a Jacob, clavó en la pared un escudo de la república que había traído consigo, y pintó en la puerta el letrero: *Corregidor*. Su primera disposición fue ordenar que todas las casas se pintaran de azul para celebrar el aniversario de la independencia nacional» (pp. 54-5). Next, religious authority takes up permanent residence in Macondo in the person of padre Nicanor Reyna «a quien don Apolinar Moscote había llevado de la ciénaga para que oficiara la boda—era un anciano endurecido por la ingratitud de su ministerio. Llevaba el propósito de regresar a su parroquia después de la boda, pero se espantó con la aridez de los habitantes de Macondo, que prosperaban en el escándalo, sujetos a la ley natural, sin bautizar a los hijos ni santificar las fiestas. Pensando que a ninguna tierra le hacía tanta falta la simiente de Dios, decidió quedarse una semana más para cristianizar a circuncisos y gentiles, legalizar concubinarios y sacramentar muribundos» (pp. 76-7). The institutionalization of Macondo mirrors the Spanish model in Latin America in which the administrative and judicial functions were not clearly defined. The governors *(corregidores)* and the municipal mayors *(alcaldes)* all served as judges. Their decisions could be reviewed by the highest court in the colonies, called the *audencia*. The privileged classes, which included the army, civil officials and the Church, had the right to be judged by their own special courts. The Church, which formed the other half of the powerful ruling structure of the Spanish empire, remains a decisive factor in Latin America today. During this time, the Church also amassed a great amount of property. The civil and religious authorities which institutionalized Latin America placed barriers between man and God and men.

The civil war is the next phase of Macondo's history, and the liberals and conservatives form the two warring factions:

> Los liberales estaban decididos a lanzarse a la guerra. Los liberales eran masones; gente de mala índole, partidaria de ahorcar a los curas, de implantar el matrimonio civil y el divorcio, de reconocer iguales derechos a los hijos naturales que a los legítimos, y de despedazar al país en un sistema federal que despojara de poderes a la autoridad suprema. Los conservadores, en cambio, que habían recibido el poder directamente de Dios, propugnaban por la estabilidad del orden público y la moral familiar; eran los defensores de la fe de Cristo, del principio de autoridad, y no estaban dispuestos a permitir que el país fuera descuartizado en entidades autónomas. (p. 88)

This description characterizes the political climate which existed in Latin America after it gained independence from Spain in the early nineteenth century.

Simon Bolívar, liberator of much of Latin America, envisioned a kind of United States of South America. He was president of Gran Colombia, a kind of confederation composed of what is now Venezuela, Colombia and Ecuador. He drafted his famous *constitución vitalicia* which was adopted in Bolivia in 1826. This constitution proved unworkable, and, through a series of wars, the great dream of Bolívar disappeared. After his death in 1830, the ruling classes, because of their inexperience in self-government, continued to maintain the socio-political system which Spain had bequeathed to them. Military force became the final arbiter, and this led to the rise of the *caudillos,* or military strongmen, who ruled much of Latin America in the post-independence era. Their chief trait was the exaltation of personal leadership, but they had little political astuteness. Their power depended mostly on the number of followers they could gather, and they ruled by force. These leaders were usually supported by different groups representing opposing beliefs during the nineteenth century:

> Usually there were two parties. Whether they called themselves conservatives or liberals, or centralists and federalists, the differences between them were much the

same from one country to another. In one camp were many of the land-owners and the higher clergy with their followers among the lower classes, who clung to the surviving features of the colonial social organization, defended the prerogatives of the Church, and distrusted democratic institutions. This group naturally included most of the ex-loyalists, and it was especially strong in cities that had formerly been centers of Spanish power. Primarily interested in the maintenance of the existing order, it tended to favor a strong centralized government and often supported military leaders of humble origin.

Opposed to the conservatives were the advocates of more advanced ideas, including a fraction of the land-owning class and many merchants and professional men, often of mixed blood, who resented the creole aristocracy's claim to social preeminence. Since the Church was on the other side, the liberals were anti-clerical. Frequently they advocated a «federal» or decentralized form of government in order to capitalize upon the jealousy of the provinces toward the capital. The position of the Church and the question of centralization or decentralization thus became the two great issues in the political struggles of the first half century of independence.[5]

As for the *caudillo,* he can be seen in Colonel Aureliano Buendía who decided to lead the liberal forces. Besides the general historical correlation between the civil war and Latin American history, there also exists a specific relationship between the civil war and Colombian history. García Márquez uses real names of towns and villages located in northeastern Colombia to evoke the movement of the civil war: «litoral del Caribe, el Cabo de la Vela, Villanueva, Guacamayal, Urumita, la Guajira y Riohacha» (p. 116). Colonel Aureliano Buendía was «devorado por los indios Motilones» (p. 116). Also mentioned are the towns of Turcurinca, Manaure and Hato Nuevo.

In *H,* the Colonel referred to the big war of 1885. In northeastern Colombia, civil war broke out in 1899 between liberal and conservative forces, and it was called «la guerra de los Mil Días»: «La primera batalla formal que hubo en la guerra de los Mil Días, fue la que tuvo lugar, una semana después de haber estallado, en el sitio del río Magadalena, entre Gamarra y Puerto Nacional, el 24 de octubre de 1899.»[6] The formal end to hostilities took place on October 24, 1902, with the signing of the peace treaty. In *CAS*, the peace treaty of Neerlandia brings the fighting to a close: «El acto se celebró a veinte kilómetros de Macondo, a la sombra de una ceiba gigantesca en torno a la cual había de fundarse más tarde el pueblo de Neerlandia» (p. 154). Neerlandia was a Dutch banana plantation where the signing of the peace treaty put an end to the Thousand Days War. The civil war reflects both the history of Latin America and Colombia.

After the introduction of the train, Macondo detaches itself from the outside world. But not before one last invader wreaks havoc. One day, a Mister Herbert stepped down from the train, and his presence remained a mystery until he sat down to eat lunch in the Buendía's house:

> Cuando llevaron a la mesa el atigrado racimo de banano que solían colgar en el comedor durante el almuerzo, /Mister Herbert/ arrancó la primera fruta sin mucho entusiasmo. Pero siguió comiendo mientras hablaba, saboreando, masticando, más bien con distracción de sabio que con deleite de buen comedor, y al terminar el primer racimo suplicó que le llevaran otro. Entonces sacó de la caja de herramientas que siempre llevaba consigo un pequeño estuche de aparatos ópticos. Con la incrédula atención de un comprador de diamantes examinó meticulosamente un banano seccionando sus partes con un estilete especial, pesándolas en un granatario de farmaceútico y calculando su envergadura con un calibrador de armero. (p. 196)

Soon the Americans invaded Macondo, establishing their banana plantations. They constructed their own city, complete with a swimming pool and modern conveniences. The American settlement was separated from Macondo by a fence. The Americans believed that the progress they brought to Macondo would make it prosper under the benevolent guidance of the Company. Their invasion parallels the phenomenon known in Latin America as «el imperialismo yanqui» which often took the form of economic exploitation. A specific historical parallel can again be drawn between the portrayal of the banana company in *CAS* and the United States' economic intervention in Latin America. The United Fruit Company had vested interests in the banana industry, and by the end of the nineteenth century, it became the leading producer and exporter of bananas. It also had plantations in the area near Aracataca, Colombia. The tableau of the banana company in *CAS,* like the civil war, coincides with general and specific history.

Another parallel can be seen in the massacre of the workers. In *CAS,* tensions soon developed between the workers and the Company. The workers demanded better living conditions and more adequate medical care. A strike followed, and martial law was declared in Macondo. One day the workers gathered at the train station to await the arrival of the military and civil commander of the province who had been assigned to mediate the dispute. The commander never arrived, but the army had placed machine guns in strategic positions in order to dominate the crowd. When the crowd was ordered to disperse, it refused, and a massacre followed in which many people were supposedly killed. This incident marked the end of the banana era in *CAS.* Historically, a similar episode did occur in Ciénaga, Colombia, in the Department of Magdalena, on December 5, 1928.

The last stage of Macondo's history presents few parallels with specific historical events. The departure of the banana company left Macondo in a state of decline: «Macondo estaba en ruinas. En los pantanos de las calles quedaban muebles despedazados, esqueletos de animales cubiertos de lirios colorados, últimos recuerdos de las hordas de advenedizos que se fugaron de Macondo tan atolondradamente como habían llegado. Las casas paradas con tanta urgencia durante la fiebre del banano, había sido abandonadas. La compañía bananera desmanteló sus instalaciones» (p. 280). Macondo presents the image of many Latin American communities which have been deceived by a false economic progress that momentarily lifted them from their isolation. After the passage of the banana fever, Macondo slipped back into its radical isolation. There is one curious event, however, which might derive from Colombian history. When Gastón returned to Macondo with his wife, Amaranta Ursula, he soon realized that she fully intended to stay there. Finally, to occupy his time, Gastón decided to establish an airmail service between Macondo and the provincial capital: «Fue por esa época que concibió la idea de establecer un servicio de correo aéreo. Mientras progresaban las gestiones, preparó un campo de aterrizaje en la antigua región encantada» (p. 323). The plane that he had ordered never arrived because his associates in Brussels had sent the plane to a tribe in Africa with a similar name. Disillusioned, Gastón decided to return to Brussels: «Cansado de esperar el aeroplano, un día metió en una maletita las cosas indispensables y su archivo de correspondencia y se fue con el propósito de regresar por el aire, antes de que sus privilegios fueran cedidos a un grupo de aviadores alemanes que habían presentado a las autoridades provinciales un proyecto más ambicioso que el suyo» (p. 340). The allusion to a group of German aviators could refer to the introduction of the airplane in Barranquilla, Colombia in 1920. The following text could be a possible source for the episode in *CAS:*

LA NAVEGACION EN ALAS

Un acontecimiento que estremeció de sorpresa y admiración al mundo, fue el invento del aeroplano.

La idea de establecer un servicio de transportes aéreos nació en la mente del industrial alemán establecido en Barranquilla, don Alberto Tietjen, y su idea contó con la buena acogida de un grupo respetable de alemanes y colombianos. El 5 de diciembre de 1919 se firmó en la Notaría 2ª de Barranquilla, la escritura de constitución de la sociedad Colombo-Alemana de Transportes Aéreos, cuya sigla, que atribuyeron a la inteligencia del doctor Abel Carbonell, quedó sintetizada en *SCADTA;* siendo sus fundadores los señores Alberto Tietjen, General Rafael María Palacio, Ernesto Cortissoz, Cristóbal Restrepo, Jacobo A. Correa, Arístides Noguera y Stuart Hosie.

Este servicio aéreo era el primero que se intentaba implantar en Colombia y en América, lo cual constituye un honor para Colombia y especialmente para Barranquilla.

Para poner en práctica tan plausible idea, alentados por la influencia de los técnicos alemanes, señores Fritz W. Hammer, W. Schnurbusch y Helmuth von Krohn, se adquirió el primer hidroavión de manufactura alemana, que empezó a hacer vuelos con solo dos pasajeros, de Barranquilla a Giradot en ocho horas, y a la capital de la República, con trasbordo, en dos días. La llegada a Barranquilla de von Krohn en 1920 fue de gran aliento.

Recuerdo que él llevó hasta Santa Marta, un hidroavión, para hacer cortos vuelos dentro de la ciudad y alrededores, a los particulares, a fin de que se probara este ejercicio en el espacio y durante varios días y con tarifa equitativa, centenares de personas volamos en ese aparato y quedamos encantados con este novísimo ejercicio. Von Krohn, que seguía haciendo viajes de Barranquilla a Santa Marta y viceversa, en una de esas travesías, yendo en compañía del banquero Jacobo Cortizos y otros respetables barranquilleros, pereció junto con sus compañeros; tragedia que fue muy lamentada. En Barranquilla se erigió un monumento recordatorio de esta catástrofe. [7]

In both *CAS* and the historical account, the project failed. Gastón abandoned his idea because the plane never arrived. In the case of von Krohn, he lost his life in a crash, and a monument was erected in Barranquilla to commemorate the disaster.

CAS provides the most complete image of Macondo and the forces which affect it. Cycles of heat and rain characterize its tropical climate, but they do not become oppressive until Macondo enters its decadent stage. During its early existence, heat and rain do not affect it. In Jose Arcadio Buendía's dream about Macondo, it will be a bustling city with houses having glass walls. He uncovers the secret of his dream when he discovers ice, and then conceives the idea of making ice blocks for building houses. Macondo would then cease to be «un lugar ardiente, cuyas bisagras y aldabas se torcían de calor, para convertirse en una ciudad invernal» (p. 28). Later, when Melquíades believes that he has found a prediction about the future of Macondo which contradicts José Arcadio Buendía's dream, he thunders that «no serán casas de vidrio sino de hielo, como yo lo soñé, y siempre habrá un Buendía por los siglos de los siglos» (p. 53). He always dreams of constructing a city which opposes the tropical climate in which it is located, and disrupts the harmony between man and nature. Macondo is an artificial creation, a product of the process of civilization. José Arcadio Buendía's dreams reveal the opposition between Man/Nature, or Civilization/Barbarity, which is so prevalent in Latin American literature. The traditional Spanish distaste for nature manifested itself in the establishment of cities which were either situated on the coasts or in the mountains. As Ricardo Gullón states: «El mito predominante en la literatura americana es el de la selva. La selva, que de puro tupida y desbordante no deja ver los árboles, simboliza mejor que cualquier otra imagen la resistencia de la naturaleza a ceder a la voluntad ordenadora del hombre. La selva es el remanente de la ante-creación, de lo informe proliferando de modo libérrimo, anterior—y hostil—a la mano reguladora del creador. La selva es el caos de la víspera, y el laberinto; como él es a la vez inerte y maligna, con inercia dañina, beligerante: acecha sin cesar a quien se aventura en ella, le desorienta y extravía, le niega la salida e, indiferente, le deja perecer.»*

The balance between Macondo and nature starts to shift after the Americans arrive and alter nature on a large scale. Rain and heat intensify, and nature becomes openly hostile to Macondo. Nature's revenge begins with the deluge which lasted four years, eleven months and two days. The inhabitants are helpless before the onslaught in which «se desempedraba el cielo en unas tempestades de estropicio, y el norte mandaba unos huracanes que desportillaron techos y derribaron paredes, y desenterraron de raíz las úlimas cepas de las plantaciones» (p. 267). The heat also intensifies as Macondo decays, and it opposes Amaranta Ursula's restorative impulses: «No era comprensible que una mujer con aquel espíritu hubiera regresado a un pueblo muerto, deprimido por el polvo y el calor» (p. 319). And later on: «En aquel Macondo olvidado hasta por los pájaros, donde el polvo y el calor se habían hecho tan tenaces que costaba trabajo respirar, recluidos por la soledad y el amor y por la soledad del amor en una casa donde era casi imposible dormir por el estruendo de las hormigas coloradas, Aureliano y Amaranta Ursula eran los únicos seres felices, y los más felices sobre la tierra» (p. 340). Rain and heat are not as prevalent in *CAS* as in his earlier works, but they are linked to the same image of Macondo in its ruined state. The rain paralyzes the inhabitants and renders all their efforts useless while the heat atrophies and chokes Macondo. Macondo has lost its place in nature by violating the tacit pact between them.

Macondo is assaulted by other plagues which constantly test its capacity to adjust. In chronological order, they are the gypsies, the insomnia and forgetfulness malady, the civil wars, the banana fever, the deluge and the other periodic intrusions of civilization. The gypsies and Melquíades bring the products of an unknown civilization which wreak havoc among Macondo's inhabitants, especially the males. They create the magical, marvelous space which installs itself in Macondo side by side with Ursula's daily space. These ordinary inventions, products of civilization and progress, surprise and disconcert Macondo's inhabitants and push José Arcadio Buendía's imagination beyond the bounds òf nature. The gypsies' visits create a series of binary oppositions which can be summarized as paradise/civilization, daily/magical reality, life/death, logic/imagination, mythical timelessness/linear time and order/disorder. Each visit helps complete the task of implanting these binary oppositions and open the way to Macondo's later entry into a different realm. Later, the gypsies again return to Macondo, but they no longer exercise any magical influence on Macondo whose own magic has disappeared.

The second plague to strike Macondo is the insomnia and forgetfulness sickness. To combat this plague, Aureliano devised a method that he discovered by chance: «Un día estaba buscando el pequeño yunque que utilizaba para laminar los metales, y no recordó su nombre. Su padre se lo dijo: 'tas.' Aureliano escribió el nombre en un papel que pegó con goma en la base del yunquecito: *tas*. Así estuvo seguro de no olvidarlo en el futuro» (p. 47). Soon José Arcadio Buendía not only labelled every object in Macondo, but described each one's use: «El letrero que colgó en la cerviz de la vaca era una muestra ejemplar de la forma en que los habitantes de Macondo estaban dispuestos a luchar contra el olvido: *Esta es la vaca, hay que ordeñarla todas las mañanas para que produzca leche y la leche hay que hervirla para mezclarla con el café y hacer café con leche*. En la entrada del camino de la ciénaga se había puesto un anuncio que decía *Macondo* y otro más grande en la calle central que decía *Dios existe*» (p. 47). The reality created by the written word cannot exist in a society based on interpersonal communication: «Así continuaron viviendo en una realidad escurridiza, momentáneamente capturada por las palabras, pero que había de fugarse sin remedio cuando olvidaran los valores de la letra escrita» (p. 47). The invention of the written word reduces personal contact by erecting a barrier between men. Macondo's history has been entirely oral up to this point, and its inhabitants do not need to record it in written form.

Macondo's inhabitants live in a primitive state where a type of primordial memory insures that they will remember their origins, and they will perish if they do not overcome the attack of forgetting. The use of writing during the plague precedes Macondo's transition from a state of atemporality and prehistory to the intervention of forces which are essentially historical (the arrival of don Apolinar Moscote who symbolizes civil authority). Macondo's primitive, timeless condition is broken by its entrance into history. In a paradoxical way, the insomnia illness, which threatened to destroy the fragile, written history completely, served instead to save it: «Esa realidad amenazada por el olvido, por una 'idiotez sin pasado', anuncia que parabólicamente la peste del insomnio la rescatará en el conocimiento, la hará tangible y viva. El pasado empieza a constituirse a partir de esa conquista de la realidad.»[9] The use of writing anticipates the moment in *CAS* when the myth of Macondo will start to coincide with recorded history. Macondo as myth will now have the arduous task of absorbing, transforming and incorporating history into its own mythical framework.

The insomnia and forgetfulness plague threatens the internal cohesion of the Buendía clan which is indissolubly linked to memory and nostalgia: «En múltiples ocasiones se reitera en la obra la importancia de los recuerdos, en ellos radica la realidad misma y cuando faltan, la realidad se desintegra. Son ellos los que le dan paso y certidumbre a los hechos vividos. El olvido es más poderoso que la muerte, el olvido determina la inexistencia misma de las cosas, no sólo en el presente, sino también en el pasado. Así el olvido de los macondinos borra la existencia de la compañía bananera, del coronel Aureliano Buendía y del crimen de la estación de ferrocarriles.»[10] The plague establishes another binary opposition between primordial and historical memories which Mircea Eliade defines respectively as the «(1) rapid and direct re-establishment of the first situation (whether Chaos or the precosmogonic state or the moment of Creation) and (2) progressive return to the 'origin' by proceeding backward in Time from the present moment to the 'absolute beginning.'»[11] The plague threatens both memories, but an inversion occurs. In order to hold on to primordial memory, Macondo's inhabitants create the primary tool for historical memory: writing. They first turn to Pilar Ternera who «concibió el artificio de leer el pasado en las barajas como antes había leído el futuro» (p. 48) José Arcadio Buendía wants to invent a memory machine which «se fundaba en la posibilidad de repasar todas las mañanas, y desde el principio hasta el fin, la totalidad de los conocimientos adquiridos en la vida» (p. 48). These acquired memories now belong to both primordial and historical memory, and the insomnia plague divides the two types of memory and puts them on different paths. Melquíades restores both types of memory: «Le dio a beber a José Arcadio Buendía una sustancia de color apacible, y la luz se hizo en su memoria» (p. 49).

The civil war and violence in *CAS* occur both in and outside of Macondo. Colombia, like many other Latin American countries, has been plagued by violence and civil war since independence, and *CAS* reflects this fact. In Colombia, after the famous «bogotazo» in 1948 when the popular leftist leader, Jorge Eliecer Gaitán, was assassinated, a wave of violence was unleashed which lasted into the 60's. It is estimated that perhaps as many as 300,000 people died, but statistics do little to soften the horrible impact of this episode. Many novelists have made violence the central focus of their works, and the «novela de la violencia» has become a literary genre. García Márquez was tempted by this genre when he wrote *La mala hora* and *El coronel no tiene quien le escriba,* but he then returned to the mythic path first indicated in *H.* Violence, resentment and hatred are present in Macondo, and they bubble to the surface in a sporadic way, but it is debatable whether violence is one of its principal features. Violence in Macondo appears in *H* when the town has been nurturing its resentment against the strange doctor for 10 years, but it remains suspended at the end of the novel. *La mala hora* is the novel to which most critics refer when they discuss violence in García Márquez' works, but he cannot be merely labelled a novelist of violence.

The civil war lasts for 20 years and sporadically touches Macondo. The war is reduced to a series of verbal communiqués which deal with the whereabouts of Colonel Aureliano Buendía. When the war breaks out, Macondo's inhabitants find out that «había estallado desde hacía tres meses. La ley marcial imperaba en todo el país» (p. 92). When Arcadio is executed, it seems justified because of his ruthless dictatorship. Macondo acts as a kind of reference point during the civil wars, but no major battles take place there. It certainly is not the center of the war, and only because Colonel Aureliano Buendía returns periodically does Macondo remain in the spotlight. Another episode of violence which occurs in Macondo concerns the massacre of the banana workers. This episode, which could be seen as a protest against political repression and Yankee imperialism, dissipates and is finally forgotten by Macondo. The only moment which might be construed as an antimilitary stance occurs when García Márquez describes the soldiers (p. 257), but he does not allow violence to overshadow his mythical perspective. He depersonalizes violence and war and thereby escapes the narrow confines of protest literature. The war becomes a kind of paradigm of all the civil wars.

The banana fever stretches Macondo's adaptive capacities to the breaking point. In Rabelaisian terms, García Márquez shows the benefits and evils of a meteoric infusion of economic progress. Macondo is first transformed then ruined by this invasion. Violence erupts again, culminating in the massacre of the banana workers. This episode could be a critique of America's economic presence in Latin America and the often disastrous results it has produced, but García Márquez does not limit himself to documenting the obvious. What is in question is the idea of civilization, and the appropriateness of Western civilization for Latin America. Progress, linear time, economic stability and development are pitted against a more *bricolage* way of doing things. Macondo's existence hangs in the balance as these two forces contend for supremacy. The United States has offered Latin America economic progress as the only viable solution to its problems. In other words, economic progress is equivalent to historical maturity, but economically, Latin America has not closed the gap. By accepting the economic imperative, Latin America has condemned itself to an endless cycle of frustration and economic disasters. As John Mander says: «America, then, is hated for what she is, not for what she does. But opinions differ as to what she is. Fundamentally, the trouble is that she is too strong, economically and militarily; and that the gap between her strength and that of Latin America has widened, not decreased, since the turn of the century.» [12] The banana fever brings the two rival ways of «progressing» into conflict, and they involve two distinct temporal patterns.

Julio Ortega distinguishes four time categories in *CAS*: «1) el mundo y el tiempo mítico de los fundadores; 2) el mundo y el tiempo histórico que introduce el coronel Aureliano Buendía y sus guerras; 3) el tiempo cíclico en la madurez y muerte de los primeros personajes, y su mundo transmutado por la inserción de Macondo en una realidad más vasta; y 4) el deterioro de Macondo, *axis mundi,* en el agotamiento del linaje, eje de Macondo.» [13] These divisions can be altered by situating the clash between mythical and linear time at the conclusion of the insomnia and forgetfulness plague, and the arrival of don Apolinar Moscote. The introduction of writing marks Macondo's entry into the linear time of history. The problem is how Macondo's mythical time coexists with linear and circular time. *CAS* opens with mythical and circular time in the first chapter, whereas the second chapter initiates the actual chronological sequence of the story of Macondo. The first two chapters correspond to Lévi-Strauss' temporal divisions of myth into historical and ahistorical. The temporal structure of the myth of Macondo has three levels. The first *(parole)* consists of the version of the myth of Macondo being recounted in *CAS*. The second *(langue)* refers to the fact that this version derives from the total myth of Macondo. The third level *(super-langue)* is the basic myth of Macondo whose fundamental components are transmitted from version to version. In terms of time, *parole* corresponds to the chronological sequence of events in *CAS*. Circular time coincides with *langue* because the different versions are repeated. Mythical time corresponds to *super-langue,* or the coded message, which is transmitted from variant to variant. Chapter 1 thus introduces *langue* and *super-langue,* and chapter 2 initiates *parole*.

This variant of the myth of Macondo narrates the entire story of Macondo from foundation to destruction. Although it takes place within an indeterminate time period, specific durations are provided for different events. The journey to establish Macondo lasts two years, Ursula is absent for five months when she goes in search of her son, Rebeca arrives on a Sunday, and the civil war lasts about 20 years. On the other hand, the reader does not know how long the insomnia plague lasts, or how long the banana company stays in Macondo. The specific-general dichotomy relativizes linear time and converts it into a flow more than a progression which can be broken down into units. Consequently, Macondo's evolution in time is much less definite, and the reader experiences a rapid, discontinuous succession of events whose alternating specificity and vagueness disrupt chronological cohesion. Chronological history becomes an illusion which Macondo's own story undermines by its very linearity. As Lévi-Strauss explains concerning history, «it cannot be represented as an aperiodic series with only a fragment of which we are acquainted. History is a discontinuous set composed of domains of history, each of which is defined by a characteristic frequency and by a differential coding of *before* and *after*. It is no more possible to pass between the dates which compose the different domains than it is to do so between natural and irrational numbers. Or more precisely: the dates appropriate to each class are irrational in relation to all those of other classes.»[14] Macondo also presents different domains of history, but no relationship exists between them. García Márquez empties every domain of its dates, and all that remains is a succession of events within each one. Linear time is an illusion in *CAS,* and the events occurring in Macondo have no *before* or *after.* Macondo waxes and wanes with the flow of events, but there is no discernible pattern of development.

Circular time pervades every level of *CAS,* and it reveals an important aspect of Latin American reality. In Latin America, linear time made a belated entry into a world in which different historical periods coexisted in the same time frame. As Alejo Carpentier explains, in «Latin America everything is outsized and disproportionate: towering mountains and waterfalls, endless plains, impenetrable jungles. An anarchic urban sprawl overlies breathless virgin expanses. The ancient rubs elbows with the new, the archaic with the futuristic, the technological with the feudal, the prehistorical with the utopic. In our cities skyscrapers stand side by side with Indian markets that sell totemic amulets.»[15] Time revolves in a circle, revealing the simultaneous presence of different epochs which linear time has discarded. As Jaime Mejía Duque says: «En resumen, *para la conciencia del hombre latinoamericano la Historia no es lineal.*»[16] It is not surprising that Macondo's atmosphere, as in *FMG,* is medieval in many respects. The gypsies bring everyday objects to Macondo which fascinate its inhabitants, and it is discovered that the earth is round. Alchemy is introduced to the Buendía men, Ursula wears a chastity belt, and the different plagues recall the Middle Ages. Macondo resembles many Latin American towns which belong to different time periods and coexist with the modern age.

García Márquez presents an image that epitomizes the overall circularity of *CAS.* A century of reading cards and experience had taught Pilar Ternera that «la historia de la familia era en engranaje de repeticiones irreparables, una rueda giratoria que hubiera seguido dando vueltas hasta la eternidad, de no haber sido por el desgaste progresivo e irremediable del eje» (p. 334). The characters are also aware of this circular, repetitive movement. Aureliano José declares: «Esta mañana, cuando me trajeron, tuve la impresion de que ya había pasado por todo esto» (p. 111). Ursula is the most conscious of circular time: «Es como si el tiempo diera vueltas en redondo y hubiéramos vuelto al principio» (p. 169); «Ursula confirmó su impresión de que el tiempo estaba dando vueltas en redondo» (p. 192); «Lo mismo que Aureliano,» exclamó Ursula. «Es como si el mundo estuviera dando vueltas» (p. 253); «Al decirlo, tuvo conciencia de estar dando la misma réplica que recibió del coronel Aureliano Buendía en su celda de sentenciado, y una vez más se estremeció con la comprobación de que el tiempo no pasaba, como ella lo acababa de admitir, sino que daba vueltas en redondo» (pp. 284-5). Despite the apparent awareness of this circular time, the spinning wheel finally wears out.

The reference to the «rueda giratoria» aptly describes *CAS*'s structure, for the wheel is immobile at its center and revolves at its perimeter. Macondo is the seat of time, the still center of the wheel, and circular time becomes the perimeter revolving around the immobile center. The rotary motion of the wheel parallels the circular movement in *CAS.* Time starts from one point and follows a curve, and, in the final stage of its trajectory, it curves back towards its initial starting point. Macondo is timeless and immobile in the sense that it is a mythical place, but the events and people rooted in Macondo follow a circular path through time. Jaime Mejía Duque describes this process in *CAS:* «Pues todo verdadero mito—y creemos aquí vernos con uno de ellos—forma como un sistema de signos profundamente coherente en sí mismo, el cual, habiendo tomado el Tiempo en cualquier punto de su devenir, lo somete de inmediato a su propia curvatura y lo torna circular. Lo cierra sobre sí. Cabría decir que, en tanto que es como una noria a la que el Tiempo se condena, cada mito es convicto sin remisión a la cosmo-idea del eterno retorno. Paradojalmente entonces por el mito es como 'este origen sin origen ni comienzo a partir del cual todo puede nacer' que es el tiempo según expresión feliz de Michel Foucault, adquiere un enorme poder germinativo para nuestra imaginación.»[17]

The written text of *CAS* presupposes the notion of repetition or circular movement. Melquíades had already written the history of Macondo and Buendía family in Sanskrit, and the narrator then told it in Spanish. This helps to explain the simultaneous presence of the future which anticipates events, such as Colonel Aureliano Buendía's execution, and the past in which the events are narrated. Cesare Segre says that time patterns in *CAS* are characterized by «la superposición de una medida temporal que mide regularmente el ritmo de los acontecimientos, y de parábolas atemporales que anticipan el futuro, o dilatan el pasado, haciendo girar a capricho la rueda del tiempo hacia los momentos cruciales del siglo de Macondo.»[18] Ursula offers a monumental symbol of the rotating wheel of time, for her life seems to span centuries: «Poco a poco se fue reduciendo, fetizándose, momificándose en vida, hasta el punto de que en sus últimos meses era una ciruela pasa perdida dentro del camisón, y el brazo siempre alzado terminó por parecer la pata de una marimonda» (p. 290). Now that the curve of her life arrives at the final stage, it bends back towards the initial starting point: «Parecía una anciana recién nacida» (p. 290). Macondo also begins to return to its point of origin when the gypsies come back again (p. 293). Amaranta Ursula commits incest with Aureliano, and their union produces a child with a pig's tail. This also closes the circle, because it fulfills the prophecy anticipated at the beginning of the novel.

Circular time in *CAS* is neutral in its treatment of all the events associated with Macondo. The civil wars repeat themselves in an endless circular pattern, and the banana fever reveals the circularity of Latin American economic history. As D. P. Gallagher says: «The phenomenon of economic boom, such as the one that attends Macondo with the advent of the banana plantation is another possible reason why a cyclical view of history predominates in Latin American writing. All over the continent there have always been booms of this kind—rubber booms, nitrate booms, gold booms, silver booms—which have provided a cycle of momentary prosperity inevitably followed by one of depression, because the mineral has run out, or foreigners have invented a cheaper synthetic alternative, or world markets have sunk.»[19] Macondo is also subject to the cycles of nature, and man's presence does little or nothing to alter these cycles. The Americans from the banana company try to reorder nature: «Dotados de recursos que en otra época estuvieron reservados a la Divina Providencia, modificaron el régimen de lluvias, apresuraron el ciclo de las cosechas, y quitaron el río de donde estuvo siempre y lo pusieron con sus piedras blancas y sus corrientes heladas en el otro extremo de la población, detrás del cementerio» (p. 197). Nature takes its revenge in *CAS*, and, as Gallagher states, «man's presence in Macondo, his history there, has turned out to be desperately fleeting. Only nature is permanent. Ultimately it is the cyclical rhythm of nature that predominates.»[20] In *CAS*, however, linear time helps destroy Macondo because it posits progress towards a goal as the ultimate good, and Macondo is much more in tune with natural cycles. Gallagher captures the essence of this circularity: «The cycles imposed by nature invalidate historical development, make history all the more an illusion, a fiction. Like Vargas Llosa's novels, *Cien años de soledad* is, as we have seen, full of the *appearance* of historical action, of apparent movement through time. Throughout the novel—on every page almost—we indeed meet adverbial phrases that suggest temporal progression: 'thirty years later,' 'it was than that,' 'afterwards.' Yet then we ask ourselves 'thirty years later' than what? When is 'then'? For this movement through time always withers in the novel's aura of timelessness, it is an illusion that only temporarily distracts from the fact that nothing changes.»[21]

Circular time is usually presented in conjunction with mythical themes, and it opens directly onto mythical time in *CAS*. The problem that arises is that if Macondo and the Buendías disappear at the end of the novel, where is the mythical Macondo which survives in another version? The answer can be found in the timeless patterns attributed to Macondo. Hans Meyerhoff says that myths «are chosen as literary symbols for two purposes: to suggest, within a secular setting, a timeless perspective of looking upon the human situation; and to convey a sense of continuity and identification with mankind in general.»[22] Macondo, despite its spatio-temporal specificity, overflows its boundaries to reveal timeless patterns. The story of Macondo is *not* the myth of Macondo, but the myth of Macondo is *every* story of Macondo. Macondo is its own beginning and end, its own repetition and its own finality. As a place in the novel, it has no extension beyond itself, but, as a mythical place, its reference points are polyvalent. Carlos Fuentes describes Macondo in the following way: «Sitio del mito: Macondo. García Márquez, fabulista, sabe que la presencia se disuelve sin un sitio (lugar de resistencias) que sea todos los sitios: un lugar que los contenga a todos, que nos contenga a todos: sede del tiempo, consagración de los tiempos, lugar de cita de la memoria y el deseo, presente común donde todo puede recomenzar: un templo, un libro.»[23] Macondo serves then as the immobile center where all the times meet, coalesce, then disperse. Each time scheme plays its role in Macondo, but mythical time synthesizes them and insures their continued existence.

Macondo is a true utopia, for it is «no place and every place,» and its foundation reflects this idea. José Arcadio Buendía dreams of a city with houses of ice (later on, of mirrors) in which there would always be a Buendía. The reader learns near the conclusion of the novel that «la ciudad de los espejos (o los espejismos) seria arrasada por el viento y desterrada de la memoria de los hombres» (p. 351). The houses made of ice suggest resistence to time, the victory of man over nature, but Macondo is also a mirage, a utopian urge, which has haunted man ever since he was ejected from paradise. Macondo, born of a dream of finding another paradise, reflects an archetypal pattern that men have repeated many times: guilt, love, expulsion, search for another place, and the persecution of innocence.[24] When José Arcadio Buendía undertakes his expedition to find civilization, his men «se sintieron abrumados por sus recuerdos más antiguos en aquel paraíso de humedad y silencio anterior al pecado original» (p. 17). And: «Varios amigos de José Arcadio Buendía, jóvenes como él, embullados con la aventura, desmantelaron sus casas y cargaron con sus mujeres y sus niños hacia la tierra que nadie les había prometido» (p. 27). This account of what led to Macondo's founding combines the myth of the «edad de oro» and the act of establishing a human settlement. Macondo's establishment takes place in a primeval setting, and it represents the union of man with nature. Octavio Paz suggests that the myth of the golden age «no está en la naturaleza ni en la historia sino entre ellas: en ese instante en que los hombres fundan su agrupación con un pacto que, simultáneamente, los une entre ellos y une al grupo con el mundo natural.»[25] García Márquez considers this vision more important than the discovery and conquest themes. Macondo, therefore, becomes a variant of the myth of the golden age, or paradise. García Márquez cannot deny the reality of the Spanish conquest, but he can limit its importance by offering another interpretation of the settlement of Latin America. His particular vision has greater authority because it is open to the modality of the mythic. If the story of Macondo were a pseudo-historical account using Aracataca as a model, or an actual historical account, its referential basis would be severely limited. Macondo's story is written in the context of timelessness where the myth of Macondo as a golden age acquires a greater scope.

René Jara plots the following temporal pattern in *CAS* which alternates between «transcurrencia y estatismo»:

a) el tiempo histórico de Riohacha y el crimen;

b) el tiempo mítico del éxodo y la fundación de Macondo;
c) el tiempo histórico de Macondo invadido por el influjo externo;
d) el tiempo mítico del retorno al caos primordial. [26]

Macondo thus becomes a mirror of Riohacha, Riohacha a mirror of Manaure, etc. The point is that Macondo, the center of mythical time, serves as a prototype for all the other cities in which the same archetypal acts have been carried out: «Se trata de hallar un lugar donde el gesto primigenio de la fundación sea posible para luego construir la propia historia, desde el comienzo.»[27] Macondo's history is no history, and every history, but it provides exemplary patterns for man's acts. Mythical time in *CAS* creates the sphere in which Macondo can exist and serve as a mediator between linear and circular time.

Macondo is thus the *bricolage* center of *CAS*. Patricia Tobin describes the process in this way: «Yet, just as surely, Márquez seems to be suggesting that the other side of historical failure is mythical hope, and the Latin America that does nothing usefully may become, through the very inutility for civilizaton of its totalizing view of man in nature, the birthing place of a sense of community, at once old and very new, that is maternal and ecological.»[28] Macondo, by its generous attitude which accepts everything, opens the door to the mythical possibilities of man's existence. García Márquez, in Macondo and *CAS*, «by rejecting the paternal guarantee of knowledge and by embracing the whole immediacy of 'everything,' he has severed the novel from its hidden alliance with knowledge and fused it once more to organic life, as it is lived beyond and before paternal deliberation.»[29] Macondo is both a place and an idea, a possibility and a realization, a unique creation and a repetition, but, above all, it is a mythical place whose function is not «*explanation* (in the sense of interpretation) but *recovery, preservation, organization, continuance,*» and whose characteristic feature is, like myth, «plenitude and accommodation, above all the accommodation of the collective mind of men to their own incessant experience.»[30]

NOTES

1. Olga Carreras González, *El mundo de Macondo en la obra de Gabriel García Már-*

quez (Miami: Ediciones Universal, 1974), p. 13.

2. *Ibid.,* pp. 16-17.

3. *Ibid.,* p. 18.

4. Gabriel García Márquez, *Isabel viendo llover en Macondo* (Buenos Aires: Editorial Estuario, 1969), p. 14. All other quotes are from this edition and will be given with page numbers in parentheses.

5. Dana Gardner Munro, *The Latin American Republics, a History* (New York: Appleton-Century-Crofts, Inc., 1951), p. 158.

6. José María Valdeblánquez, *Historia del departamento del Magdalena y del territorio de la Guajira* (Bogotá: Editorial «El Voto Nacional,» 1964), p. 27.

7. *Ibid.,* pp. 316-17.

8. Ricardo Gullón, *García Márquez o el olvidado arte de contar* (Madrid: Taurus Ediciones, S. A., 1970), pp. 45-6.

9. Julio Ortega, *La contemplación y la fiesta* (Caracas: Monte Avila Editores, S. A., 1969), p. 120.

10. González, p. 58.

11. Mircea Eliade, *Myth and Reality,* trans. Willard R. Trask (New York: Harper and Row, 1963), p. 88.

12. John Mander, *The Unrevolutionary Society* (New York: Harper and Row, 1969), p. 100.

13. Ortega, pp. 117-18.

14. Claude Lévi-Strauss, *The Savage Mind* (Chicago: The University of Chicago Press, 1970), pp. 259-60.

15. Luis Harss and Barbara Dohmann, «Alejo Carpentier, or the Eternal Return,» in *Into the Mainstream* (New York: Harper & Row, 1967), p. 39.

16. René Jara and Jaime Mejía Duque, *Las claves del mito en García Márquez* (Valparaíso: Ediciones Universitarias de Valparaíso, 1972), p. 75.

17. *Ibid.,* p. 87.

18. Cesare Segre, *Crítica bajo control,* trans. Milagros Arizmendi and María Hernández-Esteban (Barcelona: Editorial Planeta, S. A., 1970), p. 220.

19. D. P. Gallagher, *Modern Latin American Literature* (Oxford: Oxford University Press, 1973), p. 158.

20. *Ibid.,* pp. 158-9.

21. *Ibid.,* p. 159.

22. Hans Meyerhoff, *Time and Literature* (Berkeley: University of California Press, 1968), p. 80.

23. Carlos Fuentes, *La nueva novela hispanoamericana* (México: Editorial Joaquín Mortiz, S. A., 1972), p. 66.

24. Ortega, p. 119.

25. Octavio Paz, *Claude Lévi-Strauss o el nuevo festín de Esopo* (México: Joaquín Mortiz, S. A., 1969), p. 96.

26. René Jara, p. 24.

27. *Ibid.*, p. 24.

28. Patricia Drechsel Tobin, *Time and the Novel: The Genealogical Imperative* (Princeton: Princeton University Press, 1978), p. 188.

29. *Ibid.*, p. 191.

30. Warner Berthoff, *Fictions and Events: Essays in Criticism and Literary History* (New York: E. P. Dutton and Co., Inc., 1971), p. 50.

CONCLUSION

The evolution of García Márquez' fiction from *H* to *CAS* is from imitation and experimentation to originality and liberty, and it is accompanied by a progressive accessibility to to the polyvalent modalities of myth. This study confirms García Márquez' own assertion that a writer really only writes one work. Each work has been studied as an individual entity and as part of the overall development leading to *CAS* which closes the Macondo cycle, either provisionally or definitively. When García Márquez started to write *El otoño del patriarca,* he said: «Cuando me senté a escribir *El otoño del patriarca* me di cuenta de que salía igualito a *Cien años de soledad,* tenía el brazo caliente, y eso era un paseo. Concluí que tenía que desmontar por completo el estilo de *Cien años de soledad* y empezar por otro lado.»[1] García Márquez' evolution towards myth also coincides with the shift in Latin American literature from imitation to innovation. Many of the new novelists, including García Márquez, have spent much of their time abroad. This situation has produced a split between the adherents to the new novel and those who proclaim themselves committed writers. The latter accuse these expatriates of not remaining loyal to the socio-political problems of Latin America, and view them more as technical wizards than novelists reflecting contemporary Latin American reality. García Márquez went through a political phase in *El coronel no tiene quien le escriba* and *La mala hora,* but he rejected it in favor of myth. If he had devoted his energies solely to documenting the violence in Colombia, the range of his fiction would have been severely impaired. His mythical perspective encompasses Colombia, Latin America and mankind.

To accomplish his task, García Márquez uses circularity and *bricolage* which allow him to probe more deeply into the mythical reality of Latin America and of man. They open the way to «plenitude and accommodation, above all the accommodation of the collective mind of men to their own incessant experience.»[2] Circularity frees his fiction from the bonds of chronology, and amplifies the exemplary nature of man's acts. Since much of Latin America's history has legendary and mythic qualities, circularity liberates these aspects from their atrophied, chronological presentation. *Bricolage* provides a new way of studying these same events by placing the primary emphasis on arranging elements in a fluid order. These elements become expansive because of their permutability, and they retain their originality and freshness. The repetitive nausea offered by circularity is transformed into a positive factor, for *bricolage* makes it possible to renew and reshape man's archetypal acts according to the necessities of our modern age.

Bricolage also modifies the reader's relationship to the written text by bringing him into much closer contact with the orality of myth. García Márquez' mythical fiction restores the lost art of storytelling. *CAS,* like myth, succeeds in speaking narratively about significant events in an enjoyable story format. It tells this story in a mono-chromatic, nonjudgmental way which allows its audience to read/listen through the medium of the written/spoken word. This is a significant accomplishment, for, as Mircea Eliade explains, people have always felt «the need to read 'histories' and narratives that could be called paradigmtic, since they proceed in accordance with a tradi-tional model.»[3] García Márquez has also succeeded in reintroducing the storyteller of myth within the context of the modern novel. Final-ly, by putting readers in touch with myth in a narrative form, he restores the conglomerate, organic meaning of reality as revealed by man's collective experience in the world.

NOTES

1. E. González Bermejo, «Ahora 200 años de soledad,» *Oiga,* No. 392 (septiembre, 1970), p. 31.

2. Warner Berthoff, *Fictions and Events: Essays in Criticism and Literary History* (New York: E. P. Dutton and Co., Inc., 1971), p. 50.

3. Mircea Eliade, *Myth and Reality,* trans. Willard R. Trask (New York: Harper and Row, 1963), p. 191.

BIBLIOGRAPHY

Arnau, Carmen. *El mundo mítico de Gabriel García Márquez.* Barcelona: Ediciones Península, 1971.

Barthes, Roland. *Writing Degree Zero.* trans. Annette Lavers and Colin Smith. Boston: Beacon Press, 1970.

Bermejo, E. González. «Ahora 200 años de soledad.» *Oiga,* No. 392. Sept. 1970, pp. 29-32.

Berthoff, Warner. *Fictions and Events: Essays in Criticism and Literary History.* New York: Dutton, 1971.

Bodkin, Maude. *Archetypal Patterns in Poetry.* Oxford: Oxford University Press, 1950.

Briffault, Robert. *The Mothers.* New York: The Macmillan Company, 1959.

Calvino, Italo. «Myth in the Narrative.» *Surfiction: Fiction Now...and Tomorrow.* Chicago: The Swallow Press, 1975, pp. 75-81.

Cirlot, J. E. *A Dictionary of Symbols.* trans. Jack Sage. New York: Philosophical Library, 1962.

Delay, Florence, and Jaqueline de Labriolle. «Márquez est-il le Faulkner colombien?» *Revue de la littérature comparée,* 47 (1973), 88-123.

Dorfman, Ariel. «La muerte como acto imaginativo en *Cien años de soledad.» Homenaje a Gabriel García Márquez.* Ed. Helmy F. Giacoman. New York: Las Américas Publishing Company, Inc., 1972, 105-139.

Eliade, Mircea. *Cosmos and History: The Myth of the Eternal Return.* trans. Willard R. Trask. New York: Harper & Row, 1959.

Eliade, Mircea. *Myth and Reality.* trans. Willard R. Trask. New York: Harper & Row, 1963.

Fontenrose, Joseph. *The Ritual Theory of Myth.* Berkeley: University of California Press, 1971.

Fowler, Roger, *Linguistics and the Novel*. London: Methuen 1977.

Freud, Sigmund. *Totem and Taboo*. trans. James Strachey. New York: W. W. Norton, 1950.

Frye, Northrup. *Anatomy of Criticism*. Princeton: Princeton University Press, 1957.

Frye, Northrup. *Fables of Identity: Studies in Poetic Mythology*. New York: Harcourt, Brace & World, 1963.

Fuentes, Carlos. *La nueva novela hispanoamericana*. México: Editorial Joaquín Mortiz, 1969.

Gallagher, D. P. *Modern Latin American Literature*. Oxford: Oxford University Press, 1973.

García de Paredes, Franz. «Aproximación a García Márquez: *La hojarasca*.» Diss. Florida State, 1972.

García Márquez, Gabriel. *Cien años de soledad*. Buenos Aires: Editorial Sudamericana, 1967.

García Márquez, Gabriel. *Isabel viendo llover en Macondo*. Buenos Aires: Editorial Estuario, 1969.

García Márquez, Gabriel. *La hojarasca*. Buenos Aires: Editorial Sudamericana, 1969.

García Márquez, Gabriel. *La mala hora*. Buenos Aires: Editorial Sudamericana, 1969.

García Márquez, Gabriel. *Los funerales de la Mamá Grande*. Buenos Aires: Editorial Sudamericana, 1969.

García Márquez, Gabriel, and Mario Vargas Llosa. *La novela en América Latina*. Lima: Carlos Milla Batres—Ediciones Universidad Nacional de Ingeniería, 1968.

González del Valle, Luis and Vicente Cabrera. *La nueva ficción hispanoamericana*. New York: Eliseo Torres & Sons, 1972.

González, Olga Carreras. *El mundo de Macondo en la obra de Gabriel García Márquez*. Miami: Ediciones Universal, 1974.

Graves, Robert. *The Greek Myths*. Vol. 2. Baltimore: Penguin 1975.

Gullón, Ricardo. *García Márquez o el olvidado arte de contar*. Madrid: Taurus Ediciones, 1970.

Gusdorf, Georges. *Mythe et métaphysique: introduction à la philosophie*. Paris: Flammarion, 1953.

Gutiérrez Marrone, Nila. *El estilo de Juan Rulfo: estudio lingüístico*. New York: Bilingual Press, 1978.

Harss, Luis and Barbara Dohmann. «Gabriel García Márquez, or the Lost Chord.» In *Into the Mainstream*. New York: Harper & Row, 1967, pp. 310-41.

Hawkes, Terrence. *Structuralism and Semiotics*. London: Methuen 1977.

Humphrey, Robert. *Stream of Consciousness in the Modern Novel.* Berkeley: University of California Press, 1972.

Jara, René, and Jaime Mejía Duque. *Las claves del mito en García Márquez.* Valparaíso: Ediciones Universitarias de Valparaíso, 1972.

Jung, Carl G. *Man and his Symbols.* New York: Dell, 1974.

Kellogg, Robert. «Oral Literature.» *New Literary History,* Vol. V, No. 1 (Autumn, 1973), 55-66.

Kellogg, Robert and Robert Scholes. *The Nature of Narrative.* New York: Oxford University Press, 1966.

Kirk. G. S. *Myth its Meaning and Functions in Ancient and Other Cultures.* London: The Cambridge University Press, 1970.

Kumar, Shiv K. *Bergson and The Stream of Consciousness Novel.* New York: New York University Press, 1963.

Lastra, Pedro. «La tragedia como fundamento estructural de *La hojarasca.*» *In Nueve asedios a García Márquez.* Santiago: Editorial Universitaria, 1971, pp. 38-51.

Leach, Edmund. «Lévi-Strauss in the Garden of Eden: An Examination of Some Recent Developments in the Analysis of Myth.» In *Claude Lévi-Strauss: The Anthropologist as Hero.* Ed. E. Nelson and Tanya Hayes. Cambridge: The Massachusetts Institute of Technology Press, 1970, 47-60.

Lévi-Strauss, Claude. *Structural Anthropology.* trans. Claire Jacobson and Brooke Grundfest Schoepf. Garden City, New York: Doubleday, 1967.

Lévi-Strauss, Claude. *The Elementary Structures of Kinship.* trans. James Harte Bell, John Richard von Sturmer and Rodney Needham. Boston: Beacon Press, 1969.

Lévi-Strauss, Claude. *The Raw and the Cooked.* trans. John and Doreen Weightman. New York: Harper & Row, 1975.

Lévi-Strauss, Claude. *The Savage Mind.* Chicago: The University of Chicago Press, 1970.

Loveluck, Juan. «Gabriel García Márquez, narrador colombiano.» In *Nueve asedios a García Márquez.* Santiago: Editorial Universitaria, 1971, pp. 52-73.

Ludmer, Josefina. *Cien años de soledad: una interpretación.* Buenos Aires: Editorial Tiempo Contemporáneo, 1972.

Mander, John. *The Unrevolutionary Society.* New York: Harper & Row, 1969.

Martínez, Pedro Simón, ed. *Sobre García Márquez.* Montevideo: Biblioteca de Marcha, 1971.

Maturo, Graciela. *Claves simbólicas de García Márquez.* Buenos

Aires: Fernando García Cambeiro, 1972.

Mendilow, A. A. *Time and the Novel.* New York: Humanities Press, 1965.

Meyerhoff, Hans. *Time in Literature.* Berkeley: University of California Press, 1968.

Munro, Dana Gardner. *The Latin American Republics, a History.* New York: Appleton-Century-Crofts, 1951.

Neumann, Erich. *The Great Mother.* trans. Ralph Manheim. Princeton: Princeton University Press, 1963.

Ortega, Julio. *La contemplación y la fiesta.* Caracas: Monte Avila Editores, 1969.

Oviedo, José Miguel, Hugo Achugar, and Jorge Arbeleche. *Aproximación a Gabriel García Márquez.* Montevideo: Fundación de Cultura Universitaria, 1969.

Paz, Octavio. *Claude Lévi-Strauss: An Introduction.* trans. J. S. Bernstein. New York: Dell, 1979.

Paz, Octavio. *Claude Lévi-Strauss o el nuevo festín de Esopo.* México: Editorial Joaquín Mortiz, 1969.

Riencourt, Amaury de. *Sex and Power in History.* New York: Dell, 1974.

Schweitzer, S. Alan. *The Three Levels of Reality in García Márquez' Cien años de soledad.* New York: Ediciones Plaza Mayor, 1972.

Segre Cesare. *Crítica bajo control.* trans. Milagros Arizmendi and María Hernández-Esteban. Barcelona: Editorial Planeta, 1970.

Shattuck, Roger. *Marcel Proust.* New York: The Viking Press, 1974.

Shattuck, Roger. *The Banquet Years.* New York: Alfred A. Knopf, 1968.

Siemens, William L. «Tiempo, entropía y la estructura de *Cien años de soledad.*» *Explicación de Cien años de soledad.* San José, Costa Rica: Editorial Texto, 1976, pp. 359-371.

Spencer, Sharon. *Space, Time and Structure in the Modern Novel.* New York: New York University Press, 1971.

Stanzel, Franz. *Narrative Situations in the Novel.* trans. James P. Pusack. Bloomington: Indiana University Press, 1971.

Tedlock, Dennis. «Towards an Oral Poetics.» *New Literary History,* Vol. VIII, No. 3 (Spring, 1977), pp. 507-519.

The Portable Jung. Ed. Joseph Campbell. Baltimore: Penguin, 1977.

Tobin, Patricia Drechsel. *Time and the Novel: The Genealogical Imperative.* Princeton: Princeton University Press, 1978.

Todorov, Tzvetan. *The Poetics of Prose.* trans. Richard Howard. Ithaca: Cornell University Press, 1977.

Valdeblánquez, José María. *Historia del departamento del Magdalena y del territorio de la Guajira*. Bogotá: Editorial «El Voto Nacional,» 1964.

Vargas Llosa, Mario. *García Márquez: historia de un deicidio*. Barcelona: Barral Editores, 1971.

Weinrich, Harald. «Structures narratives du mythe.» *Poétique*, I (1970), pp. 25-34.

White, John J. *Mythology in the Modern Novel*. Princeton: Princeton University Press, 1971.

TABLE OF CONTENTS

Introduction 7

Overture to Myth: *La hojarasca* 15

The Mythical Transition: «Los funerales
de la Mamá Grande» 27

The *Bricolage* and Mythical Structure
of *Cien años de soledad* 39

The Banana Massacre: A Microstructural
Example of *Bricolage* and Myth 53

The Narrator of Myth and Mythical
Narration in *Cien años de soledad* 67

The Mythical Family, Characters
and *Bricolage* in *Cien
años de soledad* 93

History, Myth and Time in Macondo 121

Conclusion 147

Bibliography 149